7 Weeks to
Safe Social Drinking

7 Weeks to
Safe Social Drinking

How to Effectively Moderate
Your Alcohol Intake

Donna J. Cornett, M.A.

People Friendly Books
Santa Rosa, California

7 Weeks to Safe Social Drinking
How to Effectively Moderate Your Alcohol Intake

People Friendly Books

For information address:
People Friendly Books
P.O. Box 5441
Santa Rosa, California 95402

Originally published by Carol Publishing

ISBN: 0-9763720-0-2

Printed in the United States of America

Thanks to my parents, who gave me the freedom to realize my vision; in memory of Susan and Patty; and thanks to Carol Sampson.

Contents

Introduction

A moderate drinking revolution has taken place in the United States since this book was first published in 1997. Many health-care professionals in this country now recognize the value of a moderate drinking approach for problem drinkers. And Drink/Link Alcohol Moderation Programs, Products and Services has flourished since 1988 when it was first established. Over the years we have helped thousands of individuals and have proudly provided our services to government agencies, universities, health care professionals and organizations and businesses in the private sector. In the year 2000, we offered the groundbreaking Home Study Program—the first moderate drinking program which you can complete on your own in the privacy of your home. We offer a Telephone Counseling Program which includes weekly telephone consultations with a Drink/Link Counselor which you can conveniently arrange around your schedule. And we stand by our guarantee: If you complete a Drink/Link Program according to the instructions and continue to practice what you learn, you are guaranteed reduced alcohol consumption.

I developed Drink/Link as a result of my own problems with alcohol and my frustration with the treatment choices available to me in the United States back in the 1980s.

At the time I was stuck in a dead-end job. Struggling to make ends meet. Between relationships. Estranged from my family. Lonely and depressed and turning to alcohol for comfort. Friends thought of me as an intelligent, attractive, well-educated, and well-traveled person. I had earned a master's degree and a college teaching credential in psychology. I had lived in Europe. I had a lot going for me. But my life was falling apart and I was medicating myself with alcohol.

That was the starting point of two journeys. One personal—finding a solution I could live with for my own drinking. And one professional—finding a solution for millions of drinkers like me. A solution they could live with too.

I knew I was not a hard-core alcoholic. I had never suffered any alcohol-related problems. I rarely had a hangover, never had a DUI, and always met important obligations. Never missed work or social functions because of drinking. No one ever suggested I might be drinking too much. I never experienced health problems because of it.

My only symptoms? Psychological. I felt guilty and ashamed about how much I drank, like so many other drinkers who are concerned about their drinking but never suffer serious alcohol-related consequences. I was drinking to relieve stress and anxiety over relationships, work and money. There was no history of alcohol abuse in my family at the time. And I was health conscious. Worried about the long-term effects of heavy drinking.

I knew I was on the verge of a serious drinking problem. I figured I could "hit bottom" and let alcohol get the best of me. Or I could take charge and do something about it. Heavy drinking just did not fit into my plan for a healthy, happy life.

I also knew I was not alone in dealing with this problem. All of my friends confided in me that they too had questioned or worried about their drinking at one time or another. Some drank in response to stress or emotions. Some drank because they were party animals and drinking was expected. And some drank because that is what they had learned from parents and peers.

So I took action, first mustering up my courage then tracking down the local National Council on Alcohol Abuse office. As soon as I set foot in the place I was labeled an "alcoholic". Just being there made me an alcoholic in their eyes.

Then I dug in and started researching all of my options to treat early-stage alcohol abuse. The more I learned about the traditional treatment approach in the United States, the more I understood why drinkers in this country had no desire to seek treatment.

The traditional belief system about drinkers and drinking problems were cut and dried at the time. Any and all drinking problems were "alcoholism". Drinkers were powerless victims of the disease of alcoholism. One probably inherited a genetic predisposition for this disease. Stopping drinking forever was the only solution regardless of how serious the drinking problem was. Personal responsibility, free will and making choices did not apply to anyone with a drinking problem. This traditional belief system about drinkers and alcohol actually discouraged treatment and encouraged denial and continued drinking.

The only options available to drinkers in the 1980s were to "hit bottom" with continued drinking or stop drinking altogether with AA or an expensive treatment program. You were required to bare your soul at public meetings and believe in a "higher power" to get better. And you could never drink again. Between the belief system and the treatment options available, drinkers stayed away from help in droves and alcohol abuse raged on. No wonder it has remained a serious health, social and economic problem for decades!

"Moderate drinking" was considered a heresy at the time. Suggest the responsible use of alcohol or sensible drinking guidelines and you were considered a lunatic. Preventing a serious problem before one progressed to full-blown alcoholism had never been considered. Traditional treatment targeted only alcoholics—ten percent of the drinking population or ten to fifteen million people in the United States. It left me and the huge population of at-risk drinkers like me—90 millions people in this country—out in the cold.

"At-risk" drinkers like me were not addressed. Worried about our drinking sometimes. Afraid to talk about it for fear of being labeled "alcoholic". Ashamed of the stigma of a drinking problem. We do not consider our drinking serious enough to warrant lifelong abstinence. We do not believe in a 12 Step approach or a "higher power" to modify our drinking habits.

After much research I was convinced the belief and treatment systems were in need of an overhaul to effectively reduce the alcohol abuse rate. It was time for an affordable, commonsense and confidential approach for problem drinkers to control drinking. A "prevention" approach targeting and preventing the huge population of unaddressed at-risk drinkers from crossing the line to alcoholism. It was time to respect drinkers as individual human beings capable of change and personally responsible for their behavior, including drinking behavior. It was time to empower drinkers with safe drinking guidelines and proven behavior management strategies and techniques enabling them to manage drinking—instead of leaving drinking to chance. It was time American drinkers had access to a moderate drinking program that showed them how to modify drinking habits, reduce alcohol consumption and prevent alcoholism.

It was also time to set the record straight about drinkers and drinking problems. Not all "drinking problems" were alcoholism. Most drinkers develop a problem with alcohol over a number of years and only a small percentage of drinkers inherit a genetic predisposition for alcoholism. A moderate drinking approach can be effective for mild to moderate alcohol abusers. Drinkers still in the early stages of alcohol abuse are still capable of modifying their drinking behavior and reducing their alcohol consumption.

Drink/Link was developed in 1988 after studying hundreds of clinical studies of drinkers and moderation treatments conducted in the United States, Canada, England, Sweden, New Zealand and Australia. It was the first moderate drinking program registered with the California Department of Alcohol and Drug Programs and included in the National Directory of Drug Abuse and Alcoholism Treatment Programs published by the U.S. Department of Health and Human Services.

Drink/Link works! Over 60 percent of the drinkers who have completed the counseling program have cut their drinking in half, and over 80 percent have significantly reduced their alcohol consumption.

I am living proof the program works. I feel free—I no longer worry about my drinking. I enjoy the fun and health benefits of safe moderate drinking. A tremendous weight has been lifted off of my shoulders and I feel good about myself and my future. You too are invited to enjoy the fun, freedom and peace of mind of moderate drinking with Drink/Link.

Remember—an ounce of prevention is worth a pound of cure. You do not have to "hit bottom" before getting help for a drinking problem. Let Drink/Link be your ounce of prevention. It is your first step to addressing a drinking problem. Not your last, like abstinence and AA.

Cheers to moderate drinking and your healthier, happier life!

Donna J. Cornett, M.A.
Founder and Director
Drink/Link Alcohol Moderation Programs, Products & Services
P.O. Box 5441, Santa Rosa, CA 95402
http://www.drinklinkmoderation.com
Email: info@drinklinkmoderation.com
707-539-5465
Toll-free: 888-773-7465
Fax: 707-537-1010

The Drink/Link Moderation Program Disclaimer

Drink/Link is not recommended for the alcoholic, anyone who has a physical or psychological condition aggravated by alcohol consumption, anyone suffering from serious physical, psychological, social, legal, financial or job-related problems as a result of alcohol consumption, any woman who is pregnant or thinking of becoming pregnant, any minor, or anyone who has successfully abstained.

Results vary according to the individual.

7 Weeks to
Safe Social Drinking

1

You *Can* Take Charge of Your Drinking—Guaranteed!

*It is better to rise from life as from a banquet—
neither thirsty nor drunken.*

—Aristotle

How much richer could your life be if you took charge of your drinking and drank less?

You could feel bright and energetic every morning, look forward to a productive day, and be anxious to get to work. You'd no longer be slow and hungover. You could enjoy happier, more fulfilling relationships, knowing you're a better mate and role model to your kids because there are no more questions or concern about your drinking. You could really get ahead financially and in your career—now that your drinking isn't slowing you down and it's not an issue with your boss or colleagues. You would be able to feel good about yourself and your life instead of feeling guilty and ashamed because you think you're drinking too much or inappropriately at times. You would be really free and in charge of your life and your alcohol consumption—not the other way around. And you could savor the peace of mind that goes along with never having to worry about a drinking problem or developing alcoholism again.

How many areas of your life have been touched by your drinking? And how many would improve if you drank less?

Maybe you've never experienced any drawbacks, but you'd like to make minor adjustments—like polishing up social drinking skills, cutting your alcohol consumption during the week, or learning behavior management strategies and techniques that show you how to control your urge to drink. Or you've questioned your drinking at one time or another as most of us have, without really knowing what safe, moderate drinking is or how to achieve it. Controlling drinking behavior and staying within risk-free drinking limits would make you feel more confident, personally and professionally.

Perhaps you're interested in the health benefits associated with moderate drinking. Light drinking reduces stress. And it's a fact it can reduce the risk of heart disease. Sensible alcohol consumption can actually factor in to longer life expectancy. Moderate drinkers have been shown to outlive teetotalers and heavy drinkers. Whoever said "He who drinks one glass a day, will live to die some other way" hit the nail on the head! Even Uncle Sam has given moderate drinking thumbs-up. The U.S. Departments of Agriculture and Health and Human Services *Dietary Guidelines for Americans* acknowledges moderate drinking and the health benefits associated with it.

Whatever your reasons, a well-managed drink or two a day may be just what the doctor ordered—and could enhance the quality of your life. And these benefits can be yours with this simple moderation program.

What's Holding You Back?

What's stopping you from taking charge of your drinking?

Your first stumbling block is probably the current belief system about drinkers and alcohol—a belief system that taught you drinking was the one thing in your life you had no control over and couldn't change. Thinking that going on the wagon and AA are your only options may be another stumbling block. Like millions of other social and problem drinkers, you may feel your drinking isn't serious enough to warrant lifelong abstinence. Or the thought of baring your soul to a group of strangers about your escapades while under the influence is just too embarrassing, and daily meetings are too inconvenient. Maybe you're not particularly religious and can't buy the idea of surrendering your life to a "higher power" as required by a Twelve Step program. Or private abstinence programs are too expensive, since most run from $5,000 to $15,000 just for the initial thirty day in-patient stay. And psychotherapy may take years. Besides, you've never had the luxury of a moderation program that defines safe drinking and empowers you with clinically proven behavior management skills showing you how to control your drinking urge and stay within moderate-drinking limits.

Welcome to the club! Most of us hold at least one of these objections. Consequently, most of us continue to ignore our drinking or put off doing anything about it because we're just not ready to stop altogether and abstinence and AA seem like overkill.

Letting problem drinking slide can be dangerous though. You know the serious physical, psychological, social, financial, legal, and work-related consequences that can result from alcohol abuse. You could die from heavy drinking or lose your home, family, and job. Drinking too much and inappropriately is serious business.

Drink/Link—Your Easy First Step to Healthy Moderate Drinking

Now you can take charge of your drinking, learn responsible use of alcohol, and enjoy all of the fun, freedom, and health benefits of moderate drinking—and none of the problems—with Drink/Link!

The Drink/Link Program will help you drop bad drinking habits, learn healthy new ones, cut your alcohol consumption, and prevent alcoholism. If you catch your drinking at the first sign of a problem, you're still capable of taking control, drinking less, and eliminating the threat of alcoholism. You've still got the power to return to risk-free drinking and manage it like every other aspect of your life—like eating, exercising, and getting yourself to work on time. Problem drinking can be tackled just as we tackle heart disease, high blood pressure, and high cholesterol and addressed like any other unhealthy or unacceptable behavior—like overeating and smoking.

The fact of the matter is most drinkers graduate to alcoholism after years of problem drinking. They haven't been born with an inherited genetic predisposition for alcoholism and are not powerless victims of disease. That's why it's crucial for you to take charge of your drinking now—not later. Don't put it off until you've hit bottom and quitting is the only answer.

How does this program work? Your goal is moderate drinking—not abstinence—and you'll achieve it with this easy step-by-step program that gives you simple healthy-drinking guidelines, heightens your "drinking awareness," and empowers you with dozens of clinically proven, commonsense lifestyle, behavioral, cognitive, and motivational strategies and techniques.

Have You Got the Right Stuff to Succeed?

If you've got the right stuff and live according to the Lifestyle, Drink/Link Basics, and Behavior Management

Skills, you're guaranteed risk-free moderate drinking and reduced alcohol consumption. Let's look at the qualities that will make you a winner.

Motivation

How many psychologists does it take to change a lightbulb? Just one—but the lightbulb really has to want to change. It's an old joke, but an important lesson.

Just like the lightbulb, you'll really have to want to change to improve drinking habits and drink less. And motivation is what will see you through that change. Motivation is an intense personal desire to get something done—like learning sensible new drinking skills. It generates the energy required to apply the concepts and skills you learn every week to your actual drinking behavior.

How motivated are you? How badly do you want to break bad drinking habits and cut alcohol consumption? Think about it.

You never want to worry about serious problem drinking or alcoholism again? Want to get ahead in your career? Have better relationships with loved ones? Avoid the embarrassment and stigma that goes along with a drinking problem? Are you concerned about your health? Did a DUI cost you a fortune and your license? Want to feel good about yourself again—not guilty like the morning after a hard-drinking night?

Jot down your reasons for change. They're constant reminders of your commitment to change.

Now, on a scale from 1 to 10, with 1 being least motivated and 10 being most motivated, how motivated are you?

If you score 8 or more, there's a good chance you've got what it takes to be a winner. You'll tap into your motivation throughout the program—it will keep you on track and focused on your moderate-drinking goal.

Confidence in Your Ability to Change

How many challenges have you faced head-on and over-come? Have you followed through with a healthy new diet or exercise program? Built your business from the ground up? Worked your way through college? Bought your house after years of struggle and saving?

Each one of these challenges required a lot of hard work, sacrifice, and determination. But you ultimately achieved your goal.

You prevailed! You probably felt good about yourself too and increased your confidence in your ability to meet a challenge. And you probably felt powerful knowing you could change the course of your life.

You must feel you are the master of your destiny and capable of transforming your life if you're going to be a winner at improving your drinking behavior.

Clean Living Is a Must

Taking good care of yourself—physically and psychologically—is another prerequisite for success.

It's tough, if not impossible, to make a major lifestyle change—like learning a new drinking routine—if you're not in tip-top shape. And tip-top shape means eating a nutritional, well-balanced diet, exercising on a regular basis, getting plenty of rest, enjoying an active social life, and having lots of self-esteem. Feeling fit makes change a lot easier.

What can you do to increase your chances of success? Pay closer attention to your diet? Get more exercise? More sleep? Step up the social life? Make more money or earn that college degree—building self-esteem and self-confidence?

Get busy! Assuming personal responsibility for a happier, healthier overall lifestyle is almost as important as assuming responsibility for drinking with Drink/Link. And it will pave your way to risk-free drinking.

You've Engaged in Problem Drinking Five Years or Less

The less time you have engaged in problem drinking, the easier it will be for you to break those bad habits and replace them with new ones. The longer you have engaged in problem drinking, the longer it will take you to modify your drinking pattern and learn a new one.

If you've suffered from a drinking problem for five years or less, your chances of succeeding in the program get even better.

You Must Buy Into a New Belief System About Drinkers and Alcohol

You were "born" with a drinking problem because you inherited a genetic predisposition for it. You are not capable of changing heavy-drinking behavior because it is a disease. Any and all drinking problems are alcoholism. And abstinence and AA are the only solutions to any drinking problem.

We've been kept down by these myths for decades. And how many of us have never even considered challenging our drinking or have given up trying to change because we thought we were hopeless, helpless victims of genes and disease, must be alcoholic and incapable of change, and lifelong abstinence and AA meetings were the only ways out?

These myths may apply to a small fraction of drinkers, but not most of us. Unfortunately, though, they have discouraged us from seeking help early on, tackling our drinking, and working on a positive change—moderate drinking.

It's time you toss out these tired old notions and learn the truths about drinkers and alcohol—making it easier for you to take advantage of the program and change your drinking ways.

Researchers agree there are two different factors which can cause problem drinking: genetic predisposition and environment. Only about 20 percent of the population may have inherited a genetic predisposition making them more vulnerable to alcohol abuse. The rest of us have environmental factors to blame. Sociological and psychological factors leading us to problem drinking. The interaction between genetic predisposition and environment can also result in alcohol abuse for some drinkers. But most of us are not afflicted with an inherited tendency toward alcohol abuse. And we may drink more and more over the years and even graduate to alcoholism.

If you have two or more close relatives—parents, grandparents, brothers, sisters, aunts, or uncles—who have a problem with alcohol, you may have inherited a tendency toward alcoholism. This is all the more reason to keep an eye on your drinking and have this moderation program close at hand. Learning safe-drinking principles and skills makes sense whether you've got a family history of alcohol abuse or drink in response to the ups and downs of everyday living.

Second, about 10 percent of the drinking population suffers from the disease of alcoholism. But don't forget that before you cross the line to alcoholism, you can still break problem-drinking habits.

And not all "drinking problems" are alcoholism. In fact, drinking behavior runs on a continuum starting with social drinking to careless drinking to problem drinking and finally alcoholism. There are many different stages and forms of alcohol abuse, and any stage before alcohol dependence—"alcoholism"—is reversible. Even the *Seventh and Eighth Special Reports to the U.S. Congress on Alcohol and Health*, from the U.S. Department of Health and Human Services, published in 1990 and 1993 respectively, recognized the moderation approach that shows social and problem drinkers how to modify drinking behavior, drink less, and prevent alcoholism can work. Moderation programs in Canada, England, and Australia have shown drinkers how to master their drinking—and they can show you how to master yours.

So toss out those old notions about drinkers and alcohol that have kept you down. The truth empowers and motivates you to work this program—and modify your drinking behavior.

You Must Still Be in the Early Stages of Problem Drinking

If you don't have any problems associated with your drinking, but would like to drink less, great! But if you're facing physical, psychological, social, legal, financial, or work-related problems because of it, you need to determine how serious the problem really is.

Why is it so important to see where you fall on the continuum of drinking behavior? Because Drink/Link is most effective for the drinker who has not graduated to alcoholism. It is not recommended for the alcoholic. If you're still in the early stages of problem drinking, you're still capable of "unlearning" heavy-drinking habits and "learning" safe new ones, and the odds are greater you'll succeed in the program.

What's the difference between problem drinking and alcoholism? "Problem drinking"—alcohol abuse—can be a *psychological* dependence on alcohol. It may lead to serious health and social problems, but you don't obsess about drinking, have not developed an increased tolerance to alcohol, and do not suffer from physical withdrawal symptoms when you go without it.

"Alcoholism"—alcohol dependence—is a *psychological and physiological* dependence on alcohol. It leads to serious health and social problems, and you spend a lot of time drinking or obsessing about it, have developed a high tolerance to alcohol—requiring more and more to get high—and can't stop drinking once you've started.

Even though problem drinkers and alcoholics may suffer from some of the same symptoms, physical withdrawal symptoms indicating physiological dependence and an inability to manage drinking behavior distinguish alcoholism from problem drinking. And once you are physiologically dependent on alcohol, you are no longer in charge: Alcohol is, and it's almost impossible to modify drinking behavior. At this point, abstinence is recommended.

Let's look at your drinking from a couple of different angles. First, examine the American Psychiatric Association (APA) criteria for problem drinking and alcoholism—the standard most alcohol abuse professionals follow. Then look at the Drinking Behavior Continuum and see where you fall within it.

These two measures will give you a better understanding of the impact alcohol has had on your life and what treatment goal—moderation or abstinence—is best for you.

The American Psychiatric Association Criteria for Drinking Problems

These are the symptoms associated with problem drinking and alcoholism according to the American Psychiatric Association. Be honest with yourself and see which ones apply to you, if any.

Problem Drinking Symptoms—Alcohol Abuse*

A. A maladaptive pattern of substance use (drinking) leading to clinically significant impairment or distress, as manifested by one (or more) of the following, occurring within a twelve-month period:

*Reprinted from the American Psychiatric Association, *The Diagnostic and Statistical Manual of Mental Disorders,* 4th ed., rev., 1994.

1. recurrent alcohol use resulting in a failure to fulfill major role obligations at work, school, or home (e.g., repeated absences or poor work performance related to alcohol use; alcohol-related absences, suspensions, or expulsions from school; neglect of children or household)
2. recurrent alcohol use in situations in which it is physically hazardous (e.g., driving an automobile or operating a machine when impaired by alcohol)
3. recurrent alcohol-related legal problems (e.g., arrests for alcohol-related disorderly conduct)
4. continued alcohol use despite having persistent or recurrent social or interpersonal problems caused or exacerbated by the effects of alcohol (e.g., arguments with spouse about consequences of intoxication, physical fights)

B. The symptoms have never met the criteria for Substance Dependence for this class of substance.

Which ones apply to you? How many times over the last year have you missed work, declined a social invitation, neglected the kids or household chores, or had a spat with someone close to you because of your drinking? How many times have you driven drunk, been ticketed for being legally drunk, or had a fistfight because of alcohol?

Now look at the APA criteria for alcoholism and see how you stack up.

Alcoholism Symptoms—Alcohol Dependence*

A. A maladaptive pattern of substance use (drinking) leading to clinically significant impairment or distress, as manifested by three (or more) of the following, occurring at any time in the same twelve-month period:

*Reprinted from the American Psychiatric Assocation, *The Diagnostic and Statistical Manual of Mental Disorders,* 4th ed., rev., 1994.

1. tolerance, as defined by either of the following:
   a. a need for markedly increased amounts of alcohol to achieve intoxication or desired effect
   b. markedly diminished effect with continued use of the same amount of alcohol
2. withdrawal, as manifested by either of the following:
   a. the characteristic withdrawal syndrome for alcohol (e.g., sweating, tremors, nausea, increased pulse rate, anxiety, hallucinations or illusions, seizures)
   b. alcohol is taken to relieve or avoid withdrawal symptoms
3. alcohol is often taken in larger amounts or over a longer period than was intended
4. there is a persistent desire or unsuccessful efforts to cut down or control alcohol use
5. a great deal of time is spent in activities necessary to obtain alcohol (e.g., driving long distances), drinking, or recovering from its effects (e.g., recovering from a hangover)
6. important social, occupational, or recreational activities are given up or reduced because of drinking
7. alcohol use is continued despite knowledge of having a persistent or recurrent physical or psychological problem that is likely to have been caused or exacerbated by alcohol (e.g., continued drinking despite recognition that an ulcer was made worse by alcohol consumption)

How many times has your drinking gotten you in hot water over the last year? Do you spend a lot of time drinking or recovering from a hangover? Do you find it hard to stop drinking once you've started? How often do you wish you could cut down but have been unable to do so? Any DUIs? Are you drinking more and more and feeling the effects less and less? Are family and friends telling you your drinking is out of hand? Are you suffering from headaches, nausea, or "the shakes" if you don't drink every day? Are you drinking in the morning? Has your doctor told you to cut down or stop drinking because alcohol aggravates a medical condition?

If you're experiencing three or more symptoms, you're looking at a serious drinking problem and should consider all options—including abstinence.

Count your blessings if you don't meet the criteria for alcoholism. You may still be in the early stages of alcohol abuse, and Drink/Link could work for you.

The Drinking Behavior Continuum

Now let's look at your drinking from another angle. Check out the continuum of drinking behavior and symptoms associated with it on the next page and see where you fall.

Are you still in the social, careless, or problem drinking stages? Then you're still able to improve drinking behavior, cut alcohol consumption, and avoid alcoholism.

Still confused about how serious your drinking problem is? Schedule an evaluation with an alcohol abuse professional.

You Must Make a Sincere Commitment to Change

Are you highly motivated and confident you can change? Are you polishing up your lifestyle? Are you still in the early stages of problem drinking? Have you tossed out the old myths about drinkers and alcohol that might hold you back? Are you excited about starting the program and enhancing the quality of your life?

Congratulations! You've got what it takes to be a winner if you can honestly answer yes to these questions.

If you're ready to take the leap, buy a pocket-size notebook that you'll keep throughout the program.

DRINKING BEHAVIOR: Patterns of Use and Abuse

DEATH FROM
ALCOHOLISM

NO DRINKING

Light

Drinks less than once per month

SOCIAL

Moderate

Up to 3 drinks per occasion
"High" several times per year

Heavy

Up to 6 drinks per occasion
"High" weekly

CARELESS

When you drink, you
DRINK TOO MUCH

Minor Problems
  Family—quarrels, arguments
  Job—occasional missed work
  Money—insurance rates, fines
  Law—one arrest
  Sex—impaired performance

Hangovers that interfere with
activities

Embarrassment about things
done while drinking

PROBLEM AREA

PROBLEM

Relief drinking—to relax, calm down, sleep

Increase in tolerance

BLACKOUTS

Drinking alone or at inappropriate times

Inability to consistently predict
amount, frequency, duration, and/or
the effect of drinking

Addiction
  Changes in tolerance
  Withdrawal effects
  Morning drinks, the "eye-
    opener"
  Shakes, neglect of food
Sneaking drinks, lies, excuses
Frequent blackouts
Benders or binges
Severe health problems—
  hospitalization

ALCOHOLIC

More severe problems:
  Several arrests—legal problems
  Family complains about drinking
  Separation, divorce
  Missed work or lost jobs
  Belligerence, arguments, fights, injuries
  Money problems, unpaid bills
  Impotence, frigidity
  Health problems

REVERSIBLE PHYSIOLOGICAL DAMAGE—LIVER, STOMACH, PANCREAS, SKIN, HEART

IRREVERSIBLE PHYSIOLOGICAL DAMAGE
LIVER, BRAIN, STOMACH, PANCREAS, HEART

NO PROBLEMS RELATED TO DRINKING

YOU DO NOT HAVE TO BE AN "ALCOHOLIC"
TO HAVE A DRINKING PROBLEM

Reprinted and revised from Gayle Rosellini and Mark Warden, "The Problem Drinking Continuum," *Patterns of Use and Abuse*, Tempe, Arizona: DIN Publications.

Your first entry will be your "Commitment to Change." Promise yourself in writing to practice and complete the entire program in order—not just bits and pieces. Record your reasons for wanting to clean up your drinking act and record your goals—taking control, drinking less, enjoying the benefits of moderation, and eliminating the risk of developing alcoholism.

Get personal: Write down all the ways you could transform your life if you cut down on your drinking. No more guilt? Greater self-esteem? Getting to work on time? No more tiffs with loved ones about drinking? Less money and precious time wasted on alcohol and drinking? Feeling better than ever—physically and mentally?

Then sign and date your "Commitment to Change." Making a sincere commitment to safe drinking and focusing on your reasons for wanting to achieve it are the first steps to making it happen!

You Must Take Charge and Play an Active Role in Your Behavior Change

As Henry David Thoreau said, "Things don't change, we do." You're going to have to go out of your way to assume control and play an active role—really participate in the program—if you're going to cut down and change your drinking habits.

That means practicing the Lifestyle Basics and the Drink/Link Behavior Management Skills 100 percent of the time. It also means using your common sense and tailoring the program to your lifestyle. Personalizing the program will ensure your lasting success.

Translating these powerful tools and information into action is the only way you'll meet and maintain your moderate-drinking goal. You're the boss!

How will you put the program to work for you? First, you'll spruce up your living habits with the

Lifestyle Basics. Then you'll define "moderate drinking" and learn the Drink/Link Basics—a simple set of safe drinking guidelines.

Next, you'll heighten your "drinking awareness"—sensitizing yourself to how much you really drink, the variables that trigger your drinking "urge," and the effects of alcohol.

Each week you'll focus on a specific aspect of your drinking behavior and learn new behavior management skills—clinically proven lifestyle, behavioral, cognitive, and motivational strategies and techniques—showing you how to conquer your drinking "urge," reduce alcohol consumption, and stay within healthy drinking limits.

You're expected to practice each Drink/Link Behavior Management Skill at least three times to find out what works for you. And you must keep practicing the effective ones.

By the end of the program, you will have mastered a large repertoire of behavior management skills that enable you to change and make drinking less easy. And you will have learned a lot about yourself—especially what drives you to drink, how to break your drinking "cycle," and how to fix your problem-drinking "personality."

Most weeks you're asked to complete a simple assignment in the middle of the week. The assignment is a "teaser"—designed to give you more insight into your drinking behavior and to help you to stay on the safe-drinking track.

Allow at least one week for each chapter. You need time to digest and practice everything you learn.

You'll start with simple behavioral tips for minor adjustments to drinking behavior. Gradually you'll be asked to practice more challenging skills requiring more self-control. Don't worry—you'll be building self-control and feel confident enough to take charge and follow through with them by then.

What's that old saying? The more you give, the more you get? And the more energy you put into moderating, the more successful you'll be at controlling your drinking and shaping your future.

You Must Complete the Entire Seven-Week Program

Psychologists tell us we can break a bad habit and replace it with a good one in only three to six weeks. That's one reason why it's so important you complete the entire seven-week program in order.

At times you may feel you've got problem drinking licked, and at other times you may feel discouraged if you slip. Overcoming these ups and downs is crucial, and completing the entire program could make the difference between a permanent improvement in drinking habits and a temporary one.

You're bound to feel a little "off" in the beginning too. You may be concerned you're not enjoying the high you're used to—the first couple of weeks. That's normal. You're lowering your tolerance to alcohol.

You'll profit from it later, though: You'll discover you need a lot less alcohol to get "high" by the end of the program. So expect to feel a little off in the beginning—you're changing deeply ingrained behavior and reducing your tolerance to alcohol at the same time.

But stick with it! Just imagine how great life will be without problem drinking to worry about.

Get Ready, Get Set, Go!

Want more tips to succeeding and meeting your healthy-drinking goal?

First and foremost, focus on all the different ways you'll improve the quality of your life by moderating. A healthier, happier life is your pot of gold at the end of the rainbow.

Keeping that goal in mind will keep you motivated and on track.

Tuning in to internal and external cues that push your drinking buttons is also fundamental. The more you know about the feelings, thoughts, people, places, and circumstances that trigger your drinking urge, the more effectively you'll be able to manage them.

You could consider making a "fresh start" too. Not drinking a month before you start the program will make learning new drinking habits a cinch.

And if you're confident you can succeed in the program on your own, great! If not, consider joining or forming a Drink/Link Club for drinkers like you interested in cutting back. The emotional support you get from other drinkers who share the same safe-drinking goal could be the difference between success and failure.

Always remain patient and positive with yourself—especially if you slip from time to time. Remember, changing drinking behavior is a gradual process. It doesn't happen overnight. So get back with the program. You're the boss!

Safe drinking—and a healthier, happier life—here we come!

2

WEEK ONE: Start With the Basics

Your first week is a breeze—and so productive!

We'll look at healthy living habits—Lifestyle Basics. And how you can polish up your lifestyle to make behavior change easier. Then we'll define moderate drinking and give you safe drinking guidelines so that you'll know what you're shooting for.

You'll learn how to give yourself a passionate motivational pep talk to keep you on track and heighten your drinking awareness with your Drinking Diary and Drink Graph.

Then you'll learn your secret weapon to modifying your drinking routine—how to program your thinking and behavior before drinking with a sensible drinking plan of action.

You're laying the groundwork for moderation this week by keeping the Basics in mind, monitoring your drinking, and reprogramming your thinking and drinking habits. And you'll probably reduce alcohol consumption without even trying.

What Is Safe Drinking?

So many of us haven't a clue to what sensible drinking is. But you've got to define it before you can achieve it.

Safe drinking is moderate, appropriate drinking. "Moderate" means reasonable alcohol consumption—not excessive. And "appropriate" means drinking suited to the occasion.

It could be a couple of drinks with friends over dinner. It could be a glass or two of champagne to celebrate a special occasion. Or it could be a beer with buddies while watching a football game. Whatever the occasion, you don't go overboard and alcohol is not your primary focus. It's risk-free drinking: You no longer have to worry about risking your life, health, relationships, reputation, job, financial security, or legal status.

Safe drinking is *not* drinking as much and as fast as you can. It is not drinking until you're drunk. It never keeps you from important activities. And it never puts you or anyone else in danger.

It's not drinking because you're lonely or bored. Or drinking in response to happiness, anger, frustration—or any other emotion, for that matter. It's not drinking to satisfy hunger or thirst. Or to medicate aches and pains or use as a sleeping aid.

Safe drinking is not drinking every day because you've developed a bad habit, because you're too stressed out at work, or because everybody else is drinking too much and you've got to keep up with the crowd.

Now that you know what you're shooting for—and what you're *not* shooting for—you're halfway there!

Back to the Basics—Always

This moderation program has two gifts for you: the Lifestyle Basics—guidelines to leading a healthier, happier life—and the Drink/Link Basics—guidelines showing you how to pace yourself and stay within safe drinking limits.

Lifestyle Basics

Your first gift? Sprucing up your living habits to make better drinking habits possible. Luckily for us, the U.S. Departments of Agriculture and Health and Human Services have this all figured out. They've put together *Dietary Guidelines for Americans,** with tips on diet and exercise. Self-confidence, self-esteem, and an active social life are important too.

Diet Eat a variety of foods from the five major food groups to get the energy, protein, vitamins, minerals, and fiber you need for good health. Include plenty of fruits, vegetables, and grains. Use sugar, salt, sodium, and alcohol in moderation. And watch your cholesterol and fat.

You should choose most of your foods from the fruit, vegetable, and grain groups. A healthy diet includes two to four servings of fruit, three to five servings of vegetables, and six to eleven servings of grain products per day.

Limit yourself to two to three servings of milk products and two to three servings from the meat and bean group per day.

Watch your portions: Don't take too much!

What are the benefits of a healthy diet? Feeling better, looking better, and increased self-confidence and self-esteem.

Exercise *Dietary Guidelines for Americans* suggests thirty minutes or more of moderate exercise most days of the week.

Types of moderate exercise include brisk walking (three to four miles per hour), cleaning house, jogging, cycling, gardening, dancing, golfing, and tennis.

Need some tips to starting and sticking with an exercise program? Do something you like to do! The more fun you

*U.S. Dept. of Agriculture and U.S. Dept. of Health and Human Services, *Dietary Guidelines for Americans*, 4th ed. (Washington, D.C.: GPO, 1995).

have, the more likely it is you'll stick with it. Rollerblading? Skiing? Aerobics?

And start slow—don't overdo it. You'll be nursing aches and pains if you do too much too soon, and you'll be more likely to give up on establishing a regular exercise routine. Vary your exercise routine too. Try doing the Stairmaster on a rainy day and playing tennis on a sunny one.

What are the benefits of moderate exercise? You'll lower your blood pressure and cholesterol levels, improve cardiovascular health and lower your risk of heart disease, and come closer to your ideal weight and feel better.

Psychological Health Psychological health is just as important as physical health when it comes to maintaining a healthy, happy lifestyle. Having a good time and increasing your self-esteem are important too.

Get out and play a couple of times a week. What's your idea of fun? Hiking with a pal? Ballroom dancing? Playing touch football? Get out, socialize, and kick up your heels!

Dig into activities and tackle goals that make you feel good about yourself too. Have you been thinking about taking a class? Volunteering for a worthwhile cause? Earning more money? Switching to a more meaningful career? Go for it!

What are the benefits of getting out, having fun, and achieving? Less stress, more fun, and a rosy outlook—promoting your safe-drinking success.

What can you do to improve your physical and psychological health and enhance your quality of life? It's up to you to do it. You're in charge!

Drink/Link Basics

Amy, a successful client who is also a licensed marriage, family, and child counselor, and reaped the benefits of the

Drink/Link Basics. Even though she knew a lot about what makes people tick, she never really knew what safe drinking was or how to achieve it—like most of us. "The Drink/Link Basics have given me simple everyday guidelines for sensible drinking. I never question my drinking now—I just think of the Basics."

The Drink/Link Basics are five safe drinking guidelines to stay within moderate drinking limits. If you stick to these simple guidelines, you'll never question or worry about your drinking again. Following the Basics *is* risk-free drinking!

Another advantage of the Basics? You can have your cake and eat it too. You can enjoy light drinking but keep your blood alcohol concentration (BAC) down so that you don't get crazy. Your BAC is the amount of alcohol in your blood—the higher your BAC, the wilder you get. And keeping your BAC down enables you to exercise some self-control and practice the Drink/Link Behavior Management Skills—strategies and techniques you'll apply to modify your drinking behavior. It'll be easy for you to slow down or stop drinking—when you keep your BAC level in check with the Basics.

Basic No. 1: Enjoy only one drink per hour—no more. Nursing your drink for an hour allows you the fun of drinking and the luxury of staying in control. Most of us metabolize about one ounce of alcohol per hour—the amount of alcohol in most drinks.

So sticking to only one drink per hour means you won't get ahead of yourself and blow it. Now start timing your drinks.

Basic No. 2: Watch your drinking portions. One drink equals 1½ ounces of distilled spirits (vodka, scotch, whiskey, etc.), 5 ounces of wine, or 12 ounces of beer.

Pay attention to drinks you're pouring. You can no longer get away with pints of beer or tumblers of wine or vodka! If you're a spirits drinker, measure the alcohol in a shot glass. If you're a wine drinker, drink from a wine glass that holds only 5 ounces. And if you're a beer drinker, check the number of ounces on the container.

Start measuring today.

Basic No. 3: You're entitled up to three drinking hours on drinking days. This should allow you plenty of time to enjoy a drinking party without going overboard, considering you're observing the one-drink-per-hour Basic. Drinking more than three hours a day is a waste of your precious time.

Basic No. 4: Eat before and during drinking. This will keep your BAC down and make it easy for you to stick to the Basics. If you drink on an empty stomach, you're asking for trouble. The alcohol goes to your head, your judgment is impaired, and you've lost the ability to make sound decisions about your drinking behavior.

Basic No. 5: Plan on two or more alcohol-free days per week. Do you have days when nothing special is going on? Mondays when you head straight home from work? Days when no social event is planned? Try not drinking on these days.

You'll discover it's not that difficult after two or three tries. And it will interrupt your routine if you've fallen into a drinking habit. You may feel a bit "off" your first couple of alcohol-free days. That's natural whenever you're breaking a habit.

You know how difficult it is to stick to a new exercise routine for the first month or two? But after that, you feel comfortable with it and even miss it when there's a break in the routine? The same goes for practicing alcohol-free days. Think of yourself flexing your "self-control" muscles instead of your biceps. And the more you flex, the stronger your self-control muscles get!

After tackling the initial challenge, a couple of alcohol-free days a week will become second nature to you. It's healthy habit weaning you away from the notion that you need to drink every day.

Simple and easy—the Drink/Link Basics. Jot down the Basics in your notebook—the one you recorded your "Commitment to Change" in. And slip a copy of them in your wallet so that they're always within reach. Then commit them to memory.

Just knowing the Basics may be enough for you to stay within moderate drinking limits. If not, don't fret. The rest of your program gives you dozens of short-term and long-term strategies and techniques showing you how to stay within these boundaries and accomplish your risk-free drinking goal.

Now Set Your Limits

Establishing concrete daily and weekly drink limits will also be helpful. If you stick to the Drink/Link Basics, your maximum daily drinking limit is three drinks per day. This may be too much for you, so feel free to reduce your daily intake to one or two—whatever is best for you.

And your maximum weekly drink limit would be fifteen drinks if you followed the Basics to the letter. Five drinking days, three drinks a day. You're welcome to reduce this maximum weekly drinking limit too.

Now record your daily and weekly drinking limits in your notebook.

Estimate and record the average number of drinks you have per week prior to starting the program too. You'll refer to it at the end of the program to see how successful you've been at cutting back.

The Drink/Link Basics

1. Enjoy only one drink per hour.

2. Watch your drinking portions.

3. You're entitled to three drinking hours
on drinking days.

4. Eat before and during drinking.

5. Plan on two or more alcohol-free days per week.

Start Your Daily Drinking Diary and Weekly Drink Graph

Your Daily Drinking Diary will make you keenly aware of how much you actually drink and the variables that trigger your drinking urge and overdrinking—eventually helping you to define your "drinking personality." And your Weekly Drink Graph will monitor your progress. These are important tools you'll keep throughout the program!

Start your Drinking Diary in your notebook today. From now on, you're recording every drinking episode while working the program.

Note the start and finish of drinking times, where you were, who you were with, the occasion, how you were feeling physically (hungry? tired? thirsty?) and mentally (frustrated? happy? anxious?), how many drinks you had, your BAC level (you'll learn how to calculate this next week), the Drink/Link Behavior Management Skills you practiced and the Drink/Link Basics you managed to observe.

Set Up Your Drink/Link Drinking Diary

Day and Date Start and Finish Times	Location, Companions and Occasion	Physiological and Emotional States	Number of Drinks and BAC Level	Drink/Link Behavior Management Skills Practiced	Drink/Link Basics Observed
2/23 Friday 5:30–8	Perry's— San Francisco, Connie & Carol. Dinner out.	Starving! Uptight— lots of traffic into the city.	2 scotches .036 BAC	Delay; switched to scotch, alternate, focused on conversation, Ate.	1. 1 drink, 1 hour. 2. Eat while drinking. 3. 3 drinking hours max.
2/24 Saturday	"Alcohol-free" today— flexing my self-control muscles!				1. "Alcohol-free" day.
2/25 Sunday 6–7:30	Home, alone, making dinner.	Happy, hungry.	2 wines .052 BAC	Pacing, eating, plan to work after dinner.	1. Eat while drinking. 2. 3 drinking hours max. 3. 3 drinks max.

Set Up Your Drink/Link Weekly Drink Graph

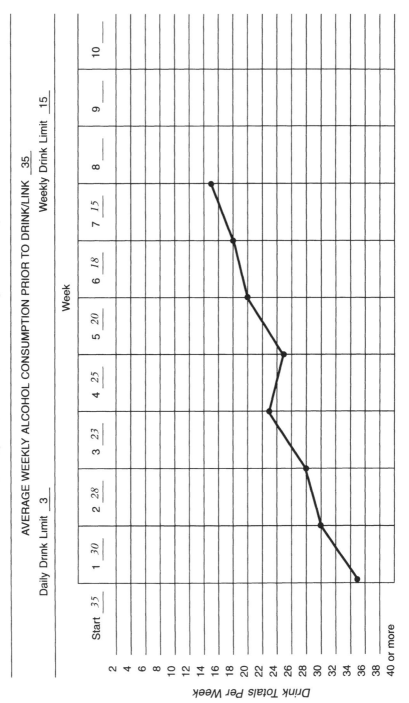

AVERAGE WEEKLY ALCOHOL CONSUMPTION PRIOR TO DRINK/LINK __35__

Daily Drink Limit __3__

Weekly Drink Limit __15__

Week

| Start 35 | 1 30 | 2 28 | 3 23 | 4 25 | 5 20 | 6 18 | 7 15 | 8 | 9 | 10 |

Drink Totals Per Week

2
4
6
8
10
12
14
16
18
20
22
24
26
28
30
32
34
36
38
40 or more

You'll start to understand why you drink and which variables to work on—if you keep your diary faithfully. And if you don't have time to record a drinking episode immediately, complete the entry as soon as possible.

Start your Weekly Drink Graph in your notebook too. Each week you'll add your daily drink totals and compare them to the weekly drink limit you've set.

Then you'll enter it on your Drink Graph—a nifty way to see how you're doing. Set up a fourteen-week graph to allow yourself seven extra weeks to keep tabs on your progress.

Check out the Daily Drinking Diary and Weekly Drink Graph for pointers on how to set them up.

Never Underestimate the Power of Your Motivational Pep Talk

"The secret of success is constancy to purpose," said Benjamin Disraeli, and he knew what he was talking about when it came to behavior change! What is your "constancy to purpose"? Your motivation—and focusing on all the reasons that get you excited about moderating.

Where will you get the energy to put the Drink/Link Behavior Management Skills you learn into action? How will you handle your drinking urge when challenged by a high-risk drinking party? What is the most important component to lasting safe-drinking success? Your motivation!

That's why your motivational pep talk is essential to your daily routine while completing the program. It's the driving force behind breaking old problem-drinking habits and replacing them with healthy new ones.

What does your pep talk consist of? It means taking ten or fifteen quiet minutes every day—long before you start drinking—and focusing on your reasons for wanting to drink less. And daydreaming about how much better your life could be—your pot of gold at the end of the rainbow—as a result of reduced alcohol consumption.

Do you look forward to feeling bright and bushy-tailed in the morning? Being a better parent to your kids? No longer worrying about becoming a slave to alcohol? No longer embarrassing yourself in front of friends and colleagues? Never again regretting things you say or do while drinking? Feeling in control of your life—having increased self-confidence and self-esteem—with less alcohol?

There could be a million different reasons behind your desire to moderate. Pinpoint them. Reflect on them every day. And feel good about yourself and get excited about your future—as a result of your sensible new drinking behavior.

Voilà! You have a passionate motivational pep talk to see you through the tough times and to sensible drinking. Just listen to your pep talk when wavering and you'll lick those heavy-drinking blues.

What quiet times during your day could you use for your pep talk? Plan on a good dose of motivation every day from now on. It's an important component of change.

Program Yourself With Your Drinking Plan of Action

What is your secret weapon to break problem-drinking habits and establish healthy new ones? Programming!

Before every drinking occasion, you'll take a break, sit quietly, and practice "programming"—helping you to formulate your drinking plan of action. What's the point of programming your thinking and drinking behavior before drinking? You'll no longer leave drinking to chance and blow it—as you have so many times in the past. You preplan and program your business day, your finances, and lots of other aspects of life. Why not be fully prepared for a drinking event?

If you know you're facing a drinking party that day, take five or ten minutes when you're not disturbed or distracted. You could be on your way to work on the bus, on your exercycle in the morning, or having lunch or an afternoon break at work. It's up to you to find time for your programming break.

Next, anticipate what that particular drinking event will be all about—who will be there, the circumstances, what you're drinking, what people will be talking about, and how you'll feel physically and mentally when you arrive.

Not all drinking events will be in social settings. Perhaps your drinking starts when you come home from work or when you're bored on a weekend. Pay special attention to high-risk drinking events that might get you in trouble.

Visualize the drinking scene. Try closing your eyes and picture yourself in the scene you've anticipated—including your feelings.

Now preplan your thinking and drinking behavior for the occasion. Will you be hungry or tired? Plan on eating something to take the edge off your appetite and to give yourself a blast of energy before you take your first drink.

Will there be any people or conversation you'll feel uncomfortable with and as a result will you resort to the comfort of alcohol? Be prepared for these feelings so you don't fall into the overdrinking trap, or consider steering clear of people or conversation that may make you anxious and trigger a drinking reaction.

How long should you stay? As long as you like, but you're allowed only three drinking hours—remember the Basics!

How much should you drink? Three drinks max—remember the Basics! When in doubt, always refer to the Basics.

The preplanning step of programming is your golden opportunity to practice all the Drink/Link Behavior Management Skills you'll learn in the program. As you complete it, you'll learn more and more strategies and techniques, so preplanning will become easier and easier.

Now rehearse your plan in your head—visualizing your preplanned drinking behavior. You'll know exactly how to handle yourself when faced with the drinking occasion. Then follow through with your drinking plan of action—the most important step of all! All the thoughts and concepts you program to modify your behavior and drink less are meaningless unless you put them to work and make changes.

Jeff worked in law enforcement but embarrassed himself when he drank socially. He always binged and made a fool of himself, which was not good for his image, to say the least. So he connected with Drink/Link.

Prior to a social event, he would sit quietly, review what he learned in the program—including the Basics—and program himself for moderate drinking that evening. He would close his eyes, picture the restaurant where he would be dining, and envision his drinking companions—working buddies. The conversation: shop talk. He'd imagine how he would be feeling physically and mentally—tired and hungry after work, intimidated by a macho drinking marathon, and anxious because he'd blown his drinking so many times before on occasions just like this.

Then he preplanned his drinking behavior for the evening. First, he knew if he snacked and had a soft drink before having a beer, he'd be less likely to fall into the bingeing trap. He'd watch the clock and pace himself—observing the Basics. After the first beer, he'd alternate with a nonalcoholic drink. And of course, he'd eat dinner—helping him keep his BAC down.

Once he realized this social occasion might turn into a drinking contest with friends, he knew he wouldn't succumb to the competitive drinking atmosphere. And he no longer felt anxious—or felt the need to medicate with alcohol—now that he programmed himself and was totally prepared for the occasion.

Finally, he followed through with his drinking plan of action. It worked! He managed that bingeing urge. And he knew if he could manage it once, he could manage it again.

Get the idea? When you've completed programming yourself with your drinking plan of action as Jeff did, you'll feel confident too. No more unplanned problem-drinking behavior or excuses!

Program Your Drinking Plan of Action

1. Sit quietly.

2. Anticipate the situation.

3. Visualize the situation.

4. Preplan your safe drinking behavior.

5. Rehearse it in your head.

6. Follow through with your drinking plan of action!

Remember the Six Programming Steps

First, sit quietly. Second, anticipate the situation. Third, visualize the situation. Fourth, preplan your safe drinking behavior. Fifth, rehearse it in your head. Finally, follow through with your drinking plan of action.

Practice makes perfect. The more you practice your programming technique, the better you'll get at it.

Your prize for practicing programming and formulating your safe-drinking plan of action before *every* drinking event? A significant reduction in alcohol consumption and improved drinking behavior—almost immediately!

Think of That Big, Beautiful Liver of Yours!

Now, there's a positive thought to include in your motivational pep talk, helping you to stay in control this week.

Can't you just picture it? That lovely liver of yours—the largest organ in your body, located in the upper right section of the abdomen—filtering blood and removing and destroying toxic substances. Imagine it secreting bile into the small intestine to help digest and absorb fat, storing vitamins, synthesizing cholesterol, and metabolizing and storing sugars. Essential to digestion and regulating blood clotting.

No liver, no life. Visualizing that great big, beautiful liver performing vital functions so efficiently could be a real motivating factor for you this first week, since you're just getting started in the program.

In fact, you could think of your two alcohol-free days every week as "Be Kind to Your Liver" days. Or visualize it when tempted to go overboard and over your drink limit. And include it in your motivational pep talk to help keep you on track and programming. Be kind to your liver—reducing your alcohol consumption—and you'll be kind to yourself!

You're the Boss—Aren't You?

You're taking control. You're totally prepared, mentally and physically, when challenged with a drinking party. You know how much and how long you'll drink. And when to slow down and stop.

Who's in charge of your drinking behavior? You or alcohol? You are! And you're playing an active role—experimenting with programming, drinking plans of action, and the Drink/Link Basics this week.

Assert yourself—and reap all of the health benefits and fun of moderation!

During the Week

How will you start each day? With your motivational pep talk, of course! Focus on your pot of gold at the end of the

---

What's Your Daily Routine While Working Drink/Link?

1. You'll start with a passionate motivational pep talk and review all your reasons for wanting to moderate and know how good your life will be when you achieve that goal.

2. You'll program yourself with a drinking plan of action and pre-plan safe drinking behavior if you're drinking that day.

3. You'll keep your Drinking Diary and record the drinking event, what behavior management skills you practiced and how much you drank.

4. You'll give yourself a pat on the back when you stick to your drinking plan of action and stay within your limits.

---

rainbow—a better life because you're drinking less. What will you do before every drinking party? Program yourself with a safe drinking plan of action and review the Basics! What will you do after your party? Record it in your Drinking Diary! And what will you do at the end of the week? Chart your progress on your Drink Graph!

Now that you've got all that under your belt, give yourself a pat on the back when you make even minor adjustments in your drinking behavior. Rewarding yourself—without alcohol—will make your transition to safe drinking easier.

What's Your Weekly Routine While Working Drink/Link?

1. You'll try to practice each one of the Drink/Link Behavior Management Skills you'll learn this week at least three times. And keep the ones that work for you.

2. You'll review your Drinking Diary and pinpoint the internal and external drinking cues that trigger your drinking urge.

3. You'll total the number of drinks you had for the week and record it on your Drink Graph.

4. You'll complete your teaser midweek.

You're just getting acquainted with brand-new concepts and skills, so be patient with yourself and remain positive. You'll get the hang of it!

No teaser this week. You've got enough to keep you busy!

Watch out! Guilt-free, risk-free drinking is right around the corner.

3

WEEK TWO: Slow Down Your Drinking—Effortlessly

Rick cut his drinking in half by the third week of the program. He was amazed at how easy it was—he did it just by slowing down and keeping the Basics in mind. He's the perfect example of a drinker who needed just a little nudge and commonsense guidelines to manage drinking.

If you can slow down your drinking, you can stay in control, remain within your drink limits, and reduce your alcohol consumption just like Rick.

This week you'll learn simple behavioral tips to do just that—effortlessly. And take baby self-control steps too, building your self-confidence and increasing your ability to manage.

Are You Up to the .06 BAC Challenge?

Your first objective this week? Keeping your blood alcohol concentration at or under .06—the "point of no return."

Why is .06 BAC called the "point of no return"? If you can stay at or under .06, you're still capable of making rational decisions about when it's time to slow down or stop drinking and putting the Drink/Link Behavior Management Skills to work for you. Once you've passed this point, you're well on your way to losing control. You can't make rational decisions and aren't interested in applying the slowing-down strategies and techniques to your drinking. And heavy, inappropriate drinking happens.

An ancient Japanese proverb may sum it up best: "First the man takes a drink, then the drink takes a drink, then the drink takes the man." You don't want to get past the point where the drink takes a drink, do you?

Look at the BAC Level Charts. How many drinks can you consume over one, two, three, and four hours that put you around .06 BAC? Make sure you look under your sex—women metabolize alcohol a little slower than men—and weight.

If you're ever questioning whether you're drinking too much or too fast, refer to the Basics. And remind yourself of the number of drinks during these specific time periods that may put you past the "point of no return"—over the .06 BAC level—and out of control. If three drinks over three hours puts you at .067, use your common sense and limit yourself to one or two drinks per day. If your weight and sex indicate you'll pass .06 BAC with three drinks over three hours its up to you to assume responsibility and make the intelligent decision to limit yourself to less alcohol—enabling you to stay under .06 BAC. Your daily limit should be one or two, but not three.

Vital information for you to know is the BAC level at which you are considered legally drunk in your state. Being ticketed for drunk driving in any state is no picnic. Besides being a danger to yourself and others, you will probably receive a huge fine, have to complete traffic school, have your license revoked and even serve jail time.

Check out the drunk-driving laws in your state. They could be powerful motivating factors for you to pace yourself—and keep you in line!

How Will You Meet the BAC Challenge and Slow Down Your Drinking?

You can stay at or under .06 BAC with really simple Drink/Link Behavior Management Skills that don't require a lot of self-control. But don't be fooled just because they're easy. The sum of these simple behavioral tips could add up to reduced alcohol consumption and safe drinking for you.

Delay That First Drink of the Day— and Successive Drinks

Good things come to those who wait. And risk-free, moderate drinking is the good thing that will come to you simply by delaying that first drink of the day by fifteen minutes or half an hour. Besides, you'll be making a powerful statement to yourself—"I'm in charge"—by putting off that first drink and spacing out the next ones.

In the beginning, glance at your watch when your drinking urge strikes. And try waiting five, ten, or fifteen minutes.

You'll get better and better at holding off, and this technique could work for up to thirty minutes. You may even graduate to a whole hour's delay.

Have a snack, take a nap, sip a soft drink—get creative and dream up something that will get your mind off drinking and delay that first drink of the day. Whatever works for you.

Putting drinking off could help you stick to the one-hour, one-drink Basic and help you stay under .06 BAC. Do it!

"Teatime," Anyone?

Taking a coffee or snack break in the late afternoon like Europeans do could give you the lift you need—and make delaying drinking painless.

If you're tempted to start drinking early in the evening, a break at about four in the afternoon might do the trick—

without alcohol. You'll quench your thirst, satisfy your hunger, and get an energy boost with coffee, tea, or juice. These are several reasons why you probably look forward to an early cocktail hour right now.

Make sense? If you can satisfy those physiological needs appropriately, you can delay and drink less.

Clean Up Those Sloppy Drinking Habits

"Years ago when I started drinking, I thought wine tasted terrible. I would take tiny sips. But over the years, I took bigger and bigger sips. Finally, I was gulping and could finish a glass of wine in fifteen minutes!" As soon as Terri started paying attention to drinking "manners," she found herself slowing down—naturally.

Have you developed sloppy drinking habits too? Do you take such big gulps that you can finish a drink in less than a half an hour? If so, you've just started drinking "charm school," devoted to teaching drinking manners and how to slow down.

Taking smaller sips—no more gulping—is easy to do, and it keeps your BAC down.

Time your sips in the beginning too. Try taking five-minute breaks between sips. Sticking to the one-drink-per-hour Basic? No problem!

Putting your drink down between sips is another trick to pace yourself. You may even forget about it at times! The more you hold on to that drink, the more likely it is that you'll drink it.

Carrying that drink with you may have become automatic over the years. Some clients have caught themselves drinking while doing laundry, watering the lawn with a drink in hand, and even cleaning house with a cocktail! Is this "appropriate" drinking behavior? Certainly not.

Are you guilty of dragging that drink around with you? If you're finding you're so attached to that cocktail that you must carry it with you at all times, it's time you start paying attention to drinking "etiquette," put the drink down, and make a difference in your alcohol consumption.

Alternate Drinks

Just alternating nonalcoholic with alcoholic drinks has made sensible drinking a snap for many clients. It doesn't take a lot of self-control, but you can stay in charge so that you know when it's time to stop. You're the boss when you alternate with mineral water, a soft drink, or a nonalcoholic beer or wine.

One of the advantages of alternating? You'll still enjoy that warm and fuzzy feeling you get from an alcoholic drink even when you're spacing them out between nonalcoholic ones.

Another advantage? Your friends won't pester you about continuing to drink with them. You're already drinking!

But the greatest advantage? You're taking charge, observing the Basics, and not going overboard.

Switch Drinks

Try drinking wine instead of that comfortable old vodka tonic or martini. Try beer instead of whiskey or brandy. Try a different type of alcoholic beverage instead of swilling down your old favorite.

You may have grown accustomed to your "usual," and you mindlessly gulp it right down. Bad news! So if you're unaccustomed to the taste of a different type of alcoholic beverage, odds are you won't gulp and will slow down.

Distract Yourself

When you're feeling the urge for a drink and want to delay it, distract yourself. If you can put off the urge and that drink for just five minutes and get involved in something else, chances are you'll forget about it for at least ten or fifteen minutes.

And knowing exactly what you'll do when the urge to drink strikes is the trick—instead of dwelling on it or feeling indecisive about what you should do instead of drinking.

Study the "101 Distractions to Keep You From Drinking" list and preplan the ones that appeal to you—then make up ten of your own.

Now when you get home from work, what will you do instead of heading straight to the refrigerator for your first beer? You'll take a shower, water your plants, love the cat, have a nonalcoholic beer, chew gum, or plan dinner. Or if you're socializing, you'll enjoy your companions, discuss topics important to you, and get involved in the activities of the occasion—not that next drink.

You're breaking a bad habit—and distracting yourself is a slick trick to slow you down and keep you under .06 BAC.

101 Distractions to Keep You From Drinking!

1. Give yourself a motivational pep talk.
2. Phone a friend.
3. Listen to music.
4. Take a walk.
5. Start writing your novel.
6. Play cards.
7. Clean out your car.
8. Give yourself a manicure.
9. Have safe sex.
10. Go to a movie.
11. Read a good book.
12. Chew gum.
13. Think up rewards for sticking to your limit.
14. Take a nap.
15. Make Chinese food.

16. Visit the local YMCA.
17. Clean out your closet.
18. Volunteer your time to your favorite charity.
19. Start a business at home.
20. Work on your garden.
21. Go window-shopping.
22. Make popcorn.
23. Plan a monthly budget.
24. Dream up alcohol-free "highs."
25. Take a drive.
26. Pay bills.
27. Watch a video.
28. Lift weights.
29. Walk your dog.
30. Make a video of yourself under the influence next time you drink.
31. Fantasize about your fantastic self-control.
32. Play the piano or guitar.
33. Balance your checkbook.
34. Read the newspaper.
35. Have a soft drink.
36. Get a massage.
37. Meditate.
38. Have a snack.
39. Knit a sweater.
40. Play with your kids or grandkids.
41. Paint a picture.
42. Explore antique shops.
43. Write a letter to a friend.
44. Take a bubble bath.
45. Floss your teeth.
46. Make Italian food.
47. Do 100 sit-ups.
48. Go to the library.
49. Play on the Internet.
50. Do a crossword puzzle.

51. Practice yoga.
52. Wash and wax your car.
53. Take a class.
54. Start a Drink/Link club.
55. Get on the Stairmaster or exercise bike.
56. Play a video game.
57. Tell a joke.
58. Redecorate.
59. Visit a friend.
60. Clean the house.
61. Give yourself a pedicure.
62. Plan your next vacation.
63. Play a game, like chess or Monopoly.
64. Become a Drink/Link Counselor.
65. Hug your teddy bear.
66. Give a massage.
67. Learn a new sport.
68. Join a social club.
69. Brainstorm ways to make money.
70. Make a batch of brownies.
71. Start a photo album.
72. Study a foreign language.
73. Start an herb garden.
74. Study more about the effects of alcohol.
75. Browse through a bookstore.
76. Sing along with your favorite CD.
77. Join a fitness club.
78. Condition your hair.
79. Love your kitty.
80. Do something nice for yourself.
81. Do something nice for your mate.
82. Get dressed up.
83. Review the Drink/Link Basics.
84. Visit that great new restaurant.
85. Engineer a stress-reduction program for yourself.
86. Loaf—do nothing.

87. Dance to your favorite music.
88. Have a cappuccino.
89. Water your plants.
90. Study tai chi.
91. Talk.
92. Listen.
93. Give yourself a facial.
94. Watch TV.
95. Become a Big Brother or Big Sister.
96. Call a Drink/Link buddy.
97. Map out your life for the next five years.
98. Eat a hot fudge sundae.
99. Fix your best friend up.
100. Pray.
101. Think about how great your life will be if you drink less.

Your Primary Focus Is People, Conversation, and Activity—Not Alcohol

A simple attitude adjustment might be in order to help you put alcohol in perspective and drink less. The less importance you assign to drinking and alcohol, the less you'll drink.

From now on, your primary focus at drinking parties is people, activity, and conversation. It may be a sporting event, dancing, or a dinner party. Get involved—you'll distract yourself and reduce your alcohol consumption.

Booze is always secondary to people and conversation— another key to slowing down. Now you're developing a healthy set of attitudes about alcohol too.

Candy Is Dandy, but Liquor Is Quicker

No kidding! That's why drinking fast is so dangerous.

Alcohol is a powerful, fast-acting drug. Treat it with respect. And never underestimate the reinforcing effect a good "high" can have on your drinking behavior—encouraging more and faster drinking.

So listen up and slow down. Keep yourself and your drinking under control.

Stay Cool—If You're Finding It Tough to Stay Within Your Limits

This is only the second week of your program. You're just getting acquainted with elementary Drink/Link Behavior Management Skills. You're just starting to flex your self-control muscles and build self-confidence. There's a lot more to come. So remain patient and positive.

And if you're finding it really tough to stay within your limits, remind yourself that it's better to bend than break. This wise advice could help you from going off the deep end in the beginning.

Compromise with yourself when confronted with a high-risk drinking party. Okay—allow yourself an extra one or two drinks—if you're not driving or doing anything physically hazardous.

Get it out of your system. But you don't have to go all out, get drunk, and give up trying to modify your drinking behavior just because you exceed your limit.

Frank, a physician, would find himself bingeing when he wasn't on call or didn't have any serious business to attend to. Consequently, he would embarrass himself and his family when drinking in casual social situations.

Compromising—especially when he first started the program—helped him to avoid excessive drinking.

Instead of giving in to splurge mentality and behavior, he programmed himself to indulge in only one or two glasses of wine over his limit—if he felt an overwhelming desire to continue drinking and wasn't doing anything important like driving or doctoring.

As he completed the program, he learned and practiced more and more behavior management skills, and developed greater confidence and self-control in risky situations. And his bingeing behavior gradually disappeared.

Compromising with himself during these high-risk drinking parties helped him stick with the program in the beginning and realize long-term moderation. And it could do the same for you too.

During the Week . . .

Have you been starting your day with a stirring motivational pep talk, focusing on your pot of gold at the end of the rainbow—a happier, healthier life with less alcohol?

How many times have you programmed yourself, followed through with your drinking plan of action and observed the Basics this week, applying all of the Drink/Link Behavior Management Skills—especially the tips for slowing down—to your drinking behavior?

Have you been reflecting on your successes so far and building self-control and self-confidence?

Record your total number of drinks for the past week on your Drink Graph. Keep up your Drinking Diary too. Which behavior management skills are working for you?

Midweek, complete your "Slow Down Your Drinking—Effortlessly" Teaser, with lots of BAC exercises.

And have fun while learning more about yourself, your drinking, and the ABCs of behavior change.

Week Two: "Slow Down Your Drinking Effortlessly" Teaser

Check out your BAC level charts. Considering your sex and body weight, how many drinks can you have during the one-, two-, three-, and four-hour intervals and still stay at or under .06 BAC? Record them. (If your BAC exceeds .06 at any time, it is up to you to immediately reduce your daily limit.)

One hour: _____
Two hours: _____
Three hours: _____
Four hours: _____

Record your BAC level for every drinking event this week, and in your Drinking Diary from now on. How often are you staying at or under .06 BAC? Are you meeting the BAC challenge?

Day one: _____
Day two: _____
Day three: _____
Day four: _____
Day five: _____
Day six: _____
Day seven: _____

How is your drinking behavior affected when you stay at or under .06 BAC?

List ten distracting activities you have preplanned to keep you from drinking when the urge strikes. And invent and record ten additional distracting activities.

What Basics and Behavior Management Skills slow you down and keep you in control?

What drinking challenges do you have coming up in the week ahead?

How will you handle them? Describe your drinking plan of action.

The following four charts are reprinted with permission from William R. Miller and Ricardo F. Munoz, *How to Control Your Drinking*, (Albuquerque: University of New Mexico Press, 1990). The titles to the charts have been slightly revised.

Approximate BAC Reached After One Hour of Drinking According to Body Weight and Number of Drinks Consumed

FOR WOMEN

Number	Body Weight							
of Drinks	100	120	140	160	180	200	220	240
1	.029	.021	.016	.012	.009	.006	.004	.002
2	.074	.058	.048	.040	.034	.028	.024	.020
3	.119	.095	.080	.068	.059	.050	.044	.038
4	.164	.132	.112	.096	.084	.072	.064	.056
5	.209	.169	.144	.124	.109	.094	.084	.074
6	.253	.206	.176	.152	.134	.116	.104	.092
7	.299	.243	.208	.180	.159	.138	.124	.110
8	.344	.280	.240	.208	.184	.160	.144	.128
9	.389	.317	.272	.236	.209	.182	.164	.146
10	.434	.354	.304	.264	.234	.204	.184	.164
11	.479	.391	.336	.292	.259	.226	.204	.182
12	.524	.428	.368	.320	.284	.248	.224	.200

FOR MEN

Number	Body Weight							
of Drinks	100	120	140	160	180	200	220	240
1	.021	.015	.011	.007	.004	.002	.001	.000
2	.058	.046	.036	.030	.024	.020	.018	.014
3	.095	.077	.062	.053	.044	.038	.035	.029
4	.132	.108	.088	.076	.064	.056	.052	.044
5	.169	.139	.114	.099	.084	.074	.069	.059
6	.206	.170	.140	.122	.104	.092	.086	.074
7	.243	.201	.166	.145	.124	.110	.103	.089
8	.280	.232	.192	.168	.144	.128	.120	.104
9	.317	.263	.218	.191	.164	.146	.137	.119
10	.354	.294	.244	.214	.184	.164	.154	.134
11	.391	.325	.270	.237	.204	.182	.171	.149
12	.428	.356	.296	.260	.224	.200	.188	.164

Approximate BAC Reached After Two Hours of Drinking According to Body Weight and Number of Drinks Consumed

FOR WOMEN

Number of Drinks	Body Weight							
	100	120	140	160	180	200	220	240
1	.013	.005	.000	.000	.000	.000	.000	.000
2	.058	.042	.032	.024	.018	.012	.008	.004
3	.103	.079	.064	.052	.043	.034	.028	.022
4	.148	.116	.096	.080	.068	.056	.048	.040
5	.193	.153	.128	.108	.093	.078	.068	.058
6	.238	.190	.160	.136	.118	.100	.088	.076
7	.283	.227	.192	.164	.143	.122	.108	.094
8	.328	.264	.224	.192	.168	.144	.128	.112
9	.373	.301	.256	.220	.193	.166	.148	.130
10	.418	.338	.288	.248	.218	.188	.168	.148
11	.463	.375	.320	.276	.243	.210	.188	.166
12	.508	.412	.352	.304	.268	.232	.208	.184

FOR MEN

Number of Drinks	Body Weight							
	100	120	140	160	180	200	220	240
1	.005	.000	.000	.000	.000	.000	.000	.000
2	.042	.030	.020	.014	.008	.004	.002	.000
3	.079	.061	.046	.037	.028	.022	.019	.013
4	.116	.092	.072	.060	.048	.040	.036	.028
5	.153	.123	.098	.083	.068	.058	.053	.043
6	.190	.154	.114	.106	.088	.076	.070	.058
7	.227	.185	.150	.129	.108	.094	.087	.073
8	.264	.216	.176	.152	.128	.112	.104	.088
9	.301	.247	.202	.175	.148	.130	.121	.103
10	.338	.278	.228	.198	.168	.148	.138	.118
11	.375	.309	.254	.221	.188	.166	.155	.133
12	.412	.340	.280	.244	.208	.184	.172	.148

Approximate BAC Reached After Three Hours of Drinking According to Body Weight and Number of Drinks Consumed

FOR WOMEN

Number of Drinks	Body Weight							
	100	120	140	160	180	200	220	240
2	.042	.026	.016	.008	.002	.000	.000	.000
3	.087	.063	.048	.036	.027	.018	.012	.006
4	.132	.100	.080	.064	.052	.040	.032	.024
5	.177	.137	.112	.092	.077	.062	.052	.042
6	.222	.174	.144	.120	.102	.084	.072	.060
7	.267	.211	.176	.148	.127	.106	.092	.078
8	.312	.248	.208	.176	.152	.128	.112	.096
9	.357	.285	.240	.204	.177	.150	.132	.114
10	.402	.322	.272	.232	.202	.172	.152	.132
11	.447	.359	.304	.260	.227	.194	.172	.150
12	.492	.396	.336	.288	.252	.216	.192	.168
13	.537	.433	.368	.316	.277	.238	.212	.186
14	.582	.470	.400	.344	.302	.260	.232	.204

FOR MEN

Number of Drinks	Body Weight							
	100	120	140	160	180	200	220	240
2	.026	.014	.004	.000	.000	.000	.000	.000
3	.063	.045	.030	.021	.012	.006	.003	.000
4	.100	.076	.056	.044	.032	.024	.020	.012
5	.137	.107	.082	.067	.052	.042	.037	.027
6	.174	.138	.108	.090	.072	.060	.054	.042
7	.211	.169	.134	.113	.092	.078	.071	.057
8	.248	.200	.160	.136	.112	.096	.088	.072
9	.285	.231	.186	.159	.132	.114	.105	.087
10	.322	.262	.212	.182	.152	.132	.122	.102
11	.359	.293	.238	.205	.172	.150	.139	.117
12	.396	.324	.264	.228	.192	.168	.156	.132
13	.433	.355	.290	.251	.212	.186	.173	.147
14	.470	.386	.316	.274	.232	.204	.190	.162

Approximate BAC Reached After Four Hours of Drinking According to Body Weight and Number of Drinks Consumed

FOR WOMEN

Number of Drinks	Body Weight							
	100	120	140	160	180	200	220	240
2	.026	.010	.000	.000	.000	.000	.000	.000
3	.071	.047	.032	.020	.011	.002	.000	.000
4	.116	.084	.064	.048	.036	.024	.016	.008
5	.161	.121	.096	.076	.061	.046	.036	.026
6	.206	.158	.128	.104	.086	.068	.056	.044
7	.251	.195	.160	.132	.111	.090	.076	.062
8	.296	.232	.192	.160	.136	.112	.096	.080
9	.341	.269	.224	.188	.161	.134	.116	.098
10	.386	.306	.256	.216	.186	.156	.136	.116
11	.431	.343	.288	.244	.211	.178	.156	.134
12	.476	.380	.320	.272	.236	.200	.176	.152
13	.521	.417	.352	.300	.261	.222	.196	.170
14	.566	.454	.384	.328	.286	.244	.216	.188
15	.611	.491	.416	.356	.311	.266	.236	.206
16	.656	.528	.448	.384	.336	.288	.256	.224

FOR MEN

Number of Drinks	Body Weight							
	100	120	140	160	180	200	220	240
2	.010	.000	.000	.000	.000	.000	.000	.000
3	.047	.029	.014	.005	.000	.000	.000	.000
4	.084	.060	.040	.028	.016	.008	.004	.000
5	.121	.091	.066	.051	.036	.026	.021	.011
6	.158	.122	.092	.074	.056	.044	.038	.026
7	.195	.153	.118	.097	.076	.062	.055	.041
8	.232	.184	.144	.120	.096	.080	.072	.056
9	.269	.215	.170	.143	.116	.098	.089	.071
10	.306	.246	.196	.166	.136	.116	.106	.086
11	.343	.277	.222	.189	.156	.134	.123	.101
12	.380	.308	.248	.212	.176	.152	.140	.116
13	.417	.339	.274	.235	.196	.170	.157	.131
14	.454	.370	.300	.258	.216	.188	.174	.146
15	.491	.401	.326	.281	.236	.206	.191	.161
16	.528	.432	.352	.304	.256	.241	.224	.176

4

Week Three: Tune in to Your Body and Brain—and Beat Your Drinking Urge

"Once I was tuned in to my urge and the thoughts and feelings surrounding it, it was a lot easier to resist it.

"I tune in to the effects of alcohol too. Now I know intuitively when to slow down or stop drinking with the Drink/Link Behavior Management Skills.

"Before I practiced Drink/Link, I would drink mindlessly. I knew I was feeling good after a couple of drinks, but didn't pay any attention to my thinking and feelings—causing me to go overboard a lot," recalls Allen, a computer whiz.

Unfortunately, most of us are like Allen—drinking carelessly and paying no attention to powerful cues that trigger our drinking urge or how we feel after a couple of drinks.

But like Allen, the more sensitive you become to your urge, what triggers it, and the physical and psychological effects of alcohol, the more likely you'll know when it's time to slow down or stop drinking.

Knowledge is power. And the more you know, the more you'll control your drinking behavior, observe the Basics, and stay within your limits.

The passwords this week? "Tune in!" Tune in to your drinking urge. Tune in to the internal and external cues telling you it's time to drink. Tune in to your ability to direct your thinking and drinking behavior. And tune in to the effects of alcohol.

Imagine yourself listening and reacting to your thinking, feelings, and bodily sensations to moderate your drinking and no longer being a slave to counting drinks!

First, Tune in to Your Drinking Urge

Oscar Wilde said, "I can resist anything but temptation." And learning how to resist or manage the temptation to start drinking or overdrink is the bottom line when it comes to modifying your drinking habits. Conquer your urge and you'll overcome problem drinking—or any other bad habit.

What is the "urge"? It's a strong desire to start or continue drinking. And it's triggered by high-risk internal and external variables. People, places, circumstances, emotional and physiological states, "drinking thinking," learned drinking behavior, and expectations about alcohol can all drive you to drink.

Your first objective this week? Tune in to your drinking urge—when and where it strikes. The more sensitive you become to it, the less susceptible you'll be to it, making it easier to manage with the behavior management skills you're learning.

The result? The urge fades, controlled drinking takes over, and you're well on your way to reduced alcohol consumption. Now when you feel that strong desire to start or continue drinking, instead of mindlessly drinking the night away, acknowledge your drinking urge.

It hit! And it's time to take a closer, deeper look at it, what's behind it, and how you're going to handle it.

Second, Tune in to the Variables That Trigger It

You're tired, hungry, and stressed-out after a rough day at work. The urge strikes.

You meet friends in a restaurant bar while you're waiting for a table for dinner. And the urge strikes.

It's five in the afternoon and a little bell goes off in your head—it's time for a drink. The urge strikes again!

These are perfect examples of drinking cues that whet your appetite for alcohol and trigger your urge.

Tuning in to specific internal and external variables is your second objective this week.

Look at external variables first—people, places, and circumstances. These are the easiest to identify, because they're tangible. You can really put your finger on them.

Then check out internal variables that set off your urge. Feelings and states of mind are more elusive, so sharpen up your sensibilities by tuning in to specific physiological, emotional, and cognitive states.

What variables push your drinking buttons according to your Daily Drinking Diary? The smarter you are about your drinking cues, the more successful you'll be at conquering the "urge" and drinking less.

Saved By a Simple Safe-Drinking Formula to Beat the Urge

How do you beat the urge? You eliminate or modify the drinking cue tripping it, or you change your reaction to it—so you don't feel an overwhelming desire to drink or over-drink.

Just plug in the behavior management skills you've learned so far and the new ones you're about to learn. And you'll beat the urge and stay in control!

How Do You Beat the Drinking Urge?

1. Eliminate the drinking cue tripping the urge.

2. Modify the drinking cue tripping the urge.

3. Change your reaction to the drinking cue.

External Drinking Triggers That Could Trip Your Urge

Hanging Out With the Wrong Crowd?   How many of your drinking buddies consider drinking parties a ritual? Family, friends, colleagues, barflies?

Certain people may get you in drinking trouble. They push alcohol on you and encourage overdrinking. They're hazardous to your health!

Isn't it high time you took charge and reduced the influence of these high-risk drinkers on your drinking behavior?

Rethink Your Drinking Relationships   Consider several different plans to lessen the influence of these high-risk drinkers.

Limit the time you spend with them—especially in the beginning of the program—and staying on track will be easier.

Keeping company with heavy drinkers while you're trying to drink less just doesn't make sense. So steer clear!

If you're really crazy about your buddies, suggest non-drinking activities, getting them and yourself away from alcohol and a drinking atmosphere.

Or turn your companions on to the moderation program. Let them know you're watching your alcohol consumption and learning healthy new drinking skills so you can manage drinking better.

Who knows? You might convert them to moderate drinking too! And instead of being challenged by these heavy-drinking pals, you could enjoy the emotional support you need to achieve your common goal—risk-free drinking. You could even form a Drink/Link Club.

Getting out and making new, sensible drinking friends could help too. Taking part in activities where alcohol is out of sight and out of mind could make a big difference in your drinking attitudes and behavior.

Your last resort if you find your buddies totally uncooperative and unwilling to support you through your behavior change and meeting your safe-drinking goal? You might have to break it off with them.

If they prove too much of a threat to your new drinking habits and you find it impossible to stay within your drink limits when you're around them, you should seriously consider ending your relationship with them.

Eliminating high-risk drinking pals and their parties could do you more good than harm. Think about it!

Do You Have a Favorite Watering Hole? One where you're always drinking (often too much) and that presents a real challenge to changing your drinking ways? A tavern next to the office? The kiosk at a sporting event? The liquor cabinet at home?

Just knowing these places push your drinking buttons will defuse their power. And here are some more suggestions to deal with them.

Get Smart—and Modify Limit the time you spend in these high-risk drinking places, especially in the beginning. The less time you spend at these hangouts, the less the urge will strike. And you won't have to deal with the urge or a heavy-drinking response.

Instead of spending two or three hours after work in the bar around the corner after work, how about just one?

You'll enjoy socializing but won't be looking at a hangover the next day.

If the kiosk at sporting events gets you in trouble, focus on the game, snacks, and nonalcoholic sodas—not on how many beers you can consume in a three-hour period.

Is drinking at home your downfall? How about delaying that first drink? Alternating with a nonalcoholic one? Distracting yourself? Safe-drinking skills that should be old friends by now—and help you manage drinking at home.

Try eating, pacing yourself, and concentrating on the activity and conversation. Brainstorm with all of the behavior management skills you've learned so far, and beat the urge in high-risk drinking locations.

Eliminate or modify the drinking cue or your reaction to it—and you'll drink less!

Do Special Circumstances Trip Your Urge?

It's five in the afternoon and the only thing you can think about is "cocktail hour."

Or you're celebrating your birthday—and give yourself permission to get smashed.

Or you've finished your work day, and a martini is an automatic response.

Or you have a whole Saturday afternoon to yourself with nothing to do—might as well treat yourself to a bottle of wine.

Or you're painting the town on Friday night—what better excuse to go all out and get drunk?

Or if the sight of alcohol or sounds of a drinking party—environmental cues—get the best of you, listen up! Unless you get a grip on these high-risk situations, breaking problem-drinking habits may be impossible.

So wise up! And take advantage of even more safe-drinking suggestions.

Don't Whine—Take Control! "Programming" your behavior and attitudes is your secret weapon when challenged with tempting situations—and mastering your urge.

Call a friend, take a brisk walk, or water your plants when the urge strikes at five. Celebrate no end—as long as you pace yourself and observe the Basics. Practice stress-reduction techniques after a rough day at work—instead of reaching for a martini. Instead of drinking your free time away on a Saturday afternoon, pamper yourself with a manicure and sauna. Dance the night away—instead of dwelling on how much and how fast you can drink because you're painting the town. And keep alcohol and drinking parties out of sight and out of mind—at least in the beginning, when you're trying to get a handle on your responsible new drinking ways.

You're the boss, aren't you?

Physiological Needs Tell You It's Drinking Time?

Have you ever caught yourself turning to alcohol because you were thirsty? Or you needed a blast of energy? Or you were hungry and alcohol took the edge off your appetite?

If you drink to satisfy basic physical needs, you're not alone. Most of us have turned to alcohol at one time or another to quench thirst, satisfy hunger, get energized, medicate pain, or put us to sleep. And it all adds up to more and more alcohol consumption throughout the week.

"I wasn't drinking enough water during the day, so as soon as I got home from work, I'd start on wine. It quenched my thirst and gave me a real lift. I drank it so fast, I'd lose control. Sometimes I'd skip dinner and often finish the whole bottle by myself in a night. And feel the effects the next day.

"Once I realized I was looking to alcohol to satisfy a couple of physical needs—more water and more energy—it was a whole lot easier to cut out drinking when I got home.

"Now I start my evening with a couple of tumblers of water, and if I'm really bushed I'll grab a ten- or fifteen-minute catnap. I sure have changed my drinking habits and drink a lot less now that I realized what I was doing," said Elizabeth, a classic example of a drinker who corrected inappropriate drinking—and reduced alcohol consumption.

How often do you drink to satisfy basic physical needs? Now when you reach for your first drink of the day, ask yourself if you're drinking to fulfill basic physiological needs, like Elizabeth. You might be surprised at the answer.

Satisfy Physiological Needs Appropriately If you're thirsty, drink water. If you're hungry, eat. If you're tired, snooze. If you're drinking to medicate aches and pains or sleep, see your physician.

It doesn't take an Einstein to figure out that if you can cut out this inappropriate drinking by gratifying these physical needs appropriately, you can reduce your overall alcohol consumption.

Does Problem Drinking Run in Your Family?

If alcohol abuse runs in your family, listen up! You may be more at risk for problem drinking and alcoholism than the average drinker.

If two or more close relatives—parents, grandparents, aunts, uncles, brothers, or sisters—have struggled with a drinking problem, chances are you could be looking at an inherited genetic predisposition for alcohol abuse too.

It's better to be safe than sorry, so you should seriously consider this wise advice: *Give alcohol and drinking your undivided attention.* Knowing you're at greater risk for alcoholism could be a blessing in disguise. You know you have to be extra careful not to fall into problem-drinking habits. All the more reason to stick with the program and pay special attention to alcohol consumption.

Knowing you've been stuck with a predisposition for alcohol abuse could be a motivating factor! It might keep you on the straight and narrow when you're tempted by the urge to go overboard.

Just think of the toll alcohol abuse has taken on other members of your family. You certainly don't want to cross the line to alcoholism and suffer the same dreadful consequences!

Are You a Slave to Learned Drinking Behavior and Expectations?

So you and your friends in high school got bombed at parties and on weekends, and you're still engaging in adolescent bingeing behavior. Or your dad sat in front of the TV when he got home from work and downed a whole six-pack of beer—every weekday night—and now you find yourself doing the same thing. Or you started drinking Scotch everyday after you landed your first big job when you graduated from college. It was a ritual you shared with your colleagues, and it was expected of you. Besides, you looked forward to melting the stress away and feeling so good in no time.

Long before you picked up your first drink, you were learning drinking habits and forming attitudes, beliefs, and expectations about drinking and alcohol which may indirectly trigger your urge.

Bringing you up, keeping you down, reducing stress, and making you feel good—all in ten or fifteen minutes! What a treat—and it's legal!

Here are some pointers to help you "unlearn" those learned attitudes and behaviors.

Set Yourself Free From Your Drinking Past   What were your parents' drinking patterns and expectations about alcohol? What habits and attitudes did you pick up from peers? What were your first experiences with alcohol? Are you stuck with the same old drinking behaviors and beliefs about alcohol you learned years ago from family and friends?

The truth will set you free. Just knowing how your drinking behavior and attitudes have been shaped by others will liberate you from them and keep you from slipping into that comfortable old drinking routine you learned so long ago.

The same goes for expectations about the effects of alcohol. Knowing that alcohol is merely a quick fix and not the means to achieving lasting bliss could dampen your enthusiasm when the urge strikes.

The more insight you gain into learned drinking behaviors, attitudes, and expectations about alcohol, the less vulnerable you'll be to them.

Do Stress and Emotions Trigger Your Urge?

Byron said, "What's drinking? A mere pause from thinking!" Do you use alcohol to pause from thinking about emotions and stress? Because you feel frustrated and there is nothing you can do about it? Or lonely and bored—and alcohol is an entertaining escape? Or because you're in the mood for a good old time? Or because you're stressed-out, angry, or anxious, and alcohol will calm you down?

Alcohol can bring you up or take you down—depending how much you drink. It can exaggerate positive or negative emotions—taking you up to the heights or down to the dregs. And stress or emotions can become powerful drinking cues for most of us at some time in our drinking career.

How often are you turning to alcohol to soothe or enhance your emotional state? Do emotional states and stress dictate your drinking behavior?

Don't turn to alcohol to cope with feelings and stress. Cope with them in healthy ways.

Address Emotions and Stress Rationally and Realistically
Instead of medicating negative emotions or getting giddy over good ones with booze, get rational and realistic.

Alcohol is only a temporary solution that will not resolve any emotional issue or diminish stress permanently. So it's time to investigate healthy alternatives for dealing with emotions or stress—not alcohol.

Problem-solve, exercise, vent your feelings, practice stress-reduction strategies and techniques. Consider professional help—see your physician, clergyman, or a licensed counselor to fix what's bugging you.

Find long-term solutions. And you could reduce your alcohol consumption.

Is "Drinking Thinking" Your Downfall?

You don't know what to have for lunch. A low-fat salad or a juicy cheeseburger?

You can't decide whether to go shopping before your exercise class or after.

You're trying to quit smoking but have an urge for a cigarette. You tell yourself you're doing everyone—including yourself—a favor by not lighting up.

These are perfect examples of inner conversation. You know, the running conversations you have with yourself telling you what you're thinking and feeling. You are weighing the pros and cons of your future actions and ultimately dictating your behavior—including drinking behavior.

Listening to your inner conversation and specifically to your "drinking thinking" tunes you in to powerful cognitive drinking cues triggering your drinking urge.

Your "drinking thinking"—a great term borrowed from the AA people—includes all the reasons and excuses you dream up to start or continue drinking, convincing yourself that drinking inappropriately and too much is okay.

"I've been so good—staying at or under my daily drink limit for two weeks now—I think I'll treat myself to a 'vacation' from the program and drink as much as I want tonight."

Or "It's my birthday! I'm having a drinking party tonight!"

Or "I've had such a rough day, to heck with the program and safe drinking."

Or "One more drink won't hurt."

These are prime examples of drinking thinking. Thoughts like these can either set off your urge or increase your awareness—telling you it's time to moderate with behavior management skills.

Direct Your Inner Conversation—and Manage Your Drinking Thinking "After a rough day at work, I thought I owed myself at least a couple of Scotches before dinner, a couple during dinner, and a couple after dinner.

"Seeing through this 'drinking thinking' helped me to cut my consumption in half. One drink before dinner and a couple of glasses of wine with dinner. I'm satisfied, don't pass .06 BAC and lose control—and I'm no longer fooling myself with lame drinking excuses," said Steven, a hot-shot lawyer.

He scored one for safe drinking when he tuned in to his inner conversation and "drinking thinking" specifically. Once he became aware of it and how to direct it, his urge was a lot easier to manage—and so was his drinking!

Want three tips to directing drinking thinking and making inner conversation work for you instead of against you? First, you've got to identify it. Second, you've got to challenge the logic behind it. And finally, you've got to talk back to it—eliminating negative inner conversation that encourages overdrinking and replacing your silly drinking excuses with positive inner conversation and affirmations. Read on. . . .

What's Your Excuse? What are your favorite forms of drinking thinking? Are they logical? Identify them and poke holes in the logic behind them. Then you can write them off—and drink less!

"I feel so good after two drinks, I'll feel even better if I keep on drinking!" How many times have you slipped into this more-is-better reasoning and had a hangover the next day? This is a popular form of drinking thinking, and one we've all engaged in at one time or another.

Maybe more exercise and more money are better. But continuing to bombard your body with more and more alcohol isn't. Recognize and get rid of this deadly drinking thinking before it gets the best of you.

"I'm so deprived, I might as well just keep on drinking." Another crazy example of drinking thinking. And so effective!

When you're feeling deprived or thinking you're not enjoying life to the fullest, you rationalize that the euphoric effects of alcohol will make up for the fun you think you're missing.

A couple of drinks—moderate drinking—will! But overindulging will make you feel bad—you'll be suffering from a hangover the next day. And it will make you feel bad about yourself when you begin to believe you have no control over alcohol or your life.

"I deserve a reward for being so good this week—I'll treat myself to a drinking party." Another favorite excuse to fall off the program and drink the way you used to.

You *do* deserve a reward for being a model safe drinker—a nonalcoholic reward—so get busy thinking some up for the next time you slip into this mindset.

"I've had such a bad day, sticking with the program is impossible today." Are you going to make a bad day worse by drinking too much and waking up with an emotional and physical hangover? Does this make sense? Of course not!

"Just one more won't hurt." How many times have you said this to yourself and gotten drunk?

"Just one more" could put you over .06 BAC—your point of no return—over your limit, and well on your way to getting drunk.

This is a lousy rationalization for reckless drinking.

"Everybody else is still drinking, so I might as well, too." "Going along with the crowd" is also a convenient excuse to overdrink.

If you think you're more socially acceptable by keeping up with your hard-drinking buddies, you're running with the wrong crowd.

"I fell off the program last night, so I might as well give up." Your conclusions about your success in the program should not be based on slipping off the program for one night.

Remember: During the process of behavior change, you're bound to slip a couple of times before you feel confident about your healthy new drinking habits.

So prepare yourself for a slip now and then. And prepare to learn from the experience and get right back on track in spite of it.

"I must finish every drink." Wrong! When you come to the sensible conclusion that you're satisfied and have reached your limit and that more drinking would be dangerous, don't sabotage yourself by telling yourself you must finish every drink.

"Waste not, want not" may be a virtuous attitudes about food and money, but not alcohol. Better to leave a little than lose control.

You may have dozens of reasons encouraging overdrinking. Maybe you think you're more fun to be with, feel better about yourself, feel sexier, more confident or glamorous, more creative or expressive. Whatever you dream up, it's time for you to pinpoint your drinking thinking and poke holes in the logic behind it.

Talk Back to Your Drinking Thinking Eliminating negative inner conversation and replacing it with positive inner conversation are two more strategies to help you overcome drinking thinking and win the war against your drinking urge.

No More Negatives   How often have you caught yourself telling yourself you can't stay on the program because it's too hard?

Or you don't want to because it's too inconvenient?

Or you won't because it deviates from your comfortable old drinking routine?

Toss out the negatives. No more "I can'ts," "I won'ts," or "don't wants." That's negative inner conversation that discourages change and fuels a bad drinking habit.

Accent the Positive   The next time you hear yourself being negative, stop! You could replace this thinking with positives instead.

You *can* meet a tough challenge. Look at some other time in your life when you rose to the challenge. It was no picnic, but you felt like a million bucks when you succeeded in meeting the challenge.

Moderating is just as important to you too. And it could change the rest of your life. So it's worth the energy and inconvenience at times.

Besides—think of that big, beautiful liver of yours and all the health benefits of limiting your alcohol consumption.

Talk back to the negatives and make them positives instead. Direct your drinking thinking and you'll direct your drinking behavior.

Finally—Tune in to the Effects of Alcohol

Beat your urge and stay in control—by getting in touch with the physical and psychological effects of alcohol when you're drinking and associating them with specific BAC levels. The more aware and sensitive you become to the effects of alcohol, the less likely you'll blow it and go overboard.

Imagine learning to judge how high you are, whether you've reached .06 BAC—the point of no return—and automatically knowing when it's time to apply your behavior management skills to your drinking behavior, making it easier and easier to moderate!

Check out these physical and psychological reactions to alcohol and the BAC levels associated with them:*

- At .02 BAC light and moderate drinkers begin to feel some effects. This is the approximate BAC reached after one drink.
- At .04 BAC most people begin to feel relaxed.
- At .06 BAC judgment is somewhat impaired; people are less likely to make rational decisions about their capabilities (e.g., to drive).
- At .08 BAC there is definite impairment of muscle coordination and driving skills; legally drunk in some states.
- At .10 BAC there is clear deterioration of reaction time and control; legally drunk in most states.
- At .12 BAC vomiting occurs, unless this level is reached slowly or the person has developed a tolerance to alcohol.
- At .15 balance and movement are impaired. This BAC level means the equivalent of one half-pint of whiskey is circulating in the bloodstream.
- At .30 many people lose consciousness.
- At .40 most people lose consciousness.
- At .45 breathing stops; fatal dose for most people.

What's going on in your head? Feeling relaxed after one drink? Think your drinking ritual permits you to let go of the ups and downs of your day?

*Reprinted from William R. Miller and Ricardo F. Munoz, *How to Control Your Drinking* (Albuquerque: University of New Mexico Press, 1990), pp. 6–7.

Feeling warm and fuzzy after two? Not a care in the world and stress is melting away? Unconcerned about how much and how fast you're drinking because you're feeling fine?

High and happy after three? You know you've reached your limit, but you start making excuses about why you should continue to drink? You know your drinking thinking has gotten you in trouble before. But you ignore it and continue drinking anyway.

You started recording your BAC levels for each drinking event in your Drinking Diary last week. Keep up the good work! And you'll get better and better at gauging how high you are and if you've reached .06 BAC—your "point of no return." Soon you won't even need BAC charts to determine your BAC.

Don't Underestimate the Power of Alcohol   Alcohol acts fast. And it doesn't take a lot to exceed .06 BAC. So be cautious—overly cautious. That way the effects of alcohol won't creep up on you, as they have in the past, and you'll stay in control.

It's a powerful drug—treat it as such!

You Can Get Full on Alcohol   When you finish a good meal, you're "full." When you reach your drink limit or .06 BAC, you're "satisfied."

This is an interesting comparison when you're sensitizing yourself to the effects of alcohol and trying to determine when to stop drinking. Think in those terms and see if it works for you.

To Drink or Not to Drink—That Is the Question   Having a tough time tuning in to the effects of alcohol and making the right decision about when it's time to slow down or stop?

Here's a surefire way to nip indecision and drinking thinking in the bud, guiding you to make the right decision and reduce your alcohol consumption. Ask yourself three questions before every drink:

1. Am I high enough?
2. Have I reached my limit?
3. Do I really want another drink?

If you answer yes to the first question, you're done! If you answer yes to the second question, you're done!

Then go to the third question. If you have answered no to questions one and two and yes to three, you may give yourself permission to have one more drink. Wasn't that easy?

This is an objective method to make the right decision whether to slow down or stop.

During the Week

What does your daily motivational pep talk sound like? Remember your reasons for wanting to drink less—and transform your life?

Keeping your Drinking Diary? You'll get so smart about the drinking cues that trigger your urge—and how to eliminate or modify them or your reaction to them—that they'll no longer pose a threat to you.

All the behavior management skills at your fingertips and ready to use? Program! Program! Program!

Are you feeling more confident and in control over drinking behavior than ever?

Record the number of drinks you've had for the week on your Drink Graph. And complete your "Why Do You Drink?" Teaser midweek.

Stay tuned! The best is yet to come.

Week Three: "Why Do You Drink?" Teaser

What external variables—people, places, and circumstances—trip your drinking urge?

What internal variables—physiological states, inherited predisposition for drinking problems, learned drinking attitudes and behaviors, expectations of alcohol, stress, emotions, and drinking thinking—trigger your urge?

What does your drinking thinking sound like?

How will you eliminate or modify your drinking cues or your reaction to them and beat your urge?

What drinking challenges are coming up for you in the next week?

Describe your drinking plans of action to overcome these challenges and stay within safe drinking limits.

5

WEEK FOUR: Turn on to Natural Highs Without Alcohol

Congratulations! You're halfway through the program. And you've earned a well-deserved "vacation"—not from programming, keeping your Drinking Diary, or practicing the behavior management skills you've learned so far, but from learning any new ones this week.

Instead, you have two fun assignments: exploring alternative ways to get "high" without alcohol and looking into rewards reinforcing your healthy new drinking habits. Replacing that warm, fuzzy feeling you get from alcohol with alcohol-free entertainment will increase your odds of moderating permanently. And rewarding yourself when you've overcome the urge and made positive changes in your drinking behavior will reinforce it.

Yes, it's still possible to have fun and get high without alcohol! You just have to investigate and pursue all of the alcohol-free activities that appeal to you.

Who says modifying drinking behavior is all work and no play?

Explore the World of Natural Highs

What natural highs—things, people, and activities—make you feel good? Put on your thinking cap and start looking into pleasures that turn you on without alcohol.

They can be simple or complicated. They can be free, cost a little, or cost a lot. You can enjoy them on your own or with other people. And they all require extra energy to go out of your way and develop alcohol-free interests.

Fact: The more time you devote to natural highs, the less importance you'll assign to alcohol and the less you'll drink.

Look to Your Past

You might start exploring your world of natural highs by reaching back in your life and thinking of the things or activities that turned you on before you got so involved with alcohol.

What did you have so much fun doing before drinking? Playing a game of tennis or chess? Eating a hot fudge sundae? Indulging in safe sex? Attending the symphony or visiting a museum? Volunteering your time to a worthwhile cause—like Big Brothers or Sisters, politics, or religion?

Sara loved playing basketball in high school and formed a basketball team for baby boomers. Jeff went to a famous cooking school—he loved to cook. And Hal volunteered his time at the YMCA—he got a kick out of kids.

Look back and think about what gave you so much pleasure before alcohol. Maybe these interests will be just as much fun as they were before. If not, continue to investigate.

Look to Your Future

This is your golden opportunity to look into activities and entertainment that you've always been interested in but never had the time or energy to pursue.

Are you interested in writing or sketching—or any other artistic endeavor—but never had the time? Like to learn to play the piano or guitar? Fascinated with tai chi but could never fit it into your schedule? Want a regular workout routine and think joining a gym sounds like fun? Now you've got the time!

Thought mountain biking or golfing looked like a good time? Or learning the art of Thai cooking? Or redecorating your house on a shoestring? Or simply baking a batch of chocolate chip cookies? Have you forgotten the fine art of just loafing? The possibilities are endless.

If you've been stuck in the house or the bar because you're chained to your drinking routine, or if you feel too lazy after a couple of drinks to get out and get interested in alcohol-free activities—like going to a movie or concert or taking a class or even a walk—you'll have to change your ways.

Putting energy into nondrinking activities will pay off. Not only will you reduce your alcohol consumption, you'll enjoy a happier, healthier life!

Get creative, like a number of clients in the program. Phil finally had the time to restore the old motorcycle in his garage. Maria treated herself to a facial and mud bath every week—really pampering herself. And Gary joined a singles group that went on outdoor adventures.

What's on Your Agenda?

Brainstorm! Think of the things that turned you on in the past and activities you always looked forward to doing. Now you've got the time and energy to do them.

Promise yourself to follow up on them too—at least three in the coming weeks—and see what tickles your fancy. Look at your schedule right now and fit them in!

Opening yourself up to new physical, social, and intellectual "highs" without alcohol will take the edge off of your urge to drink and put alcohol in the proper persepctive.

Give Yourself a Pat on the Back
When You Stick to the Program

What goodies do you have planned when you overcome a challenge—beating the urge and staying within your limits?

Reinforcing your brand-new drinking habits with a pat on the back is crucial if you expect to maintain them permanently. So it's time to get with the program—and look into treats that will help you stay on track.

The Best Things in Life Are Free or Inexpensive

How about awarding yourself gold stars for the days you stick to your drink limit? Dinner out when you stay within your weekly limit? A walk in the park, a nap on a lazy afternoon, just loafing—doing nothing at all? These are a few things you could consider when dreaming up rewards for a job well done.

Writing your novel, digging in your herb garden, swimming, baking—all of these are free activities that could be in your future.

A double decaf latte at that great new coffeehouse? Going to a matinee or visiting the aquarium or zoo—something you haven't done for years? Finally starting that paperback novel or indulging in a sinful sweet? These are inexpensive gifts that make you feel good and could help you to stick with the program.

It could be picnicking in the park—like Susan—or driving in the country—like Kurt. Cultivating simple rewards when you manage your urge and drink less could be one of the keys to your success.

Or the Best Things in Life Could Be Expensive

Some drinkers find a spectacular reward—like a Hawaiian vacation or a new mountain bike—even more effective at helping them stay on track when challenged with a dangerous drinking party.

They think big, and when the going gets tough, they imagine what a great time they're going to have doing nothing on the beach or zigzagging the countryside on their new bike. It really revives their motivation, and they realize their moderate-drinking goal.

Upgrading your computer? A diamond ring? Joining a country club? A Caribbean cruise? Which one of these spectacular rewards would motivate you to make the right choices in high-risk drinking situations?

Stan spent ten days on the beach in Mexico when he completed the program. Sam and Susan—a married couple working the program together—treated themselves to a Broadway play and a romantic night in a nice hotel. And Lisa had a big party honoring herself for sticking to the program and making the safe-drinking grade.

You deserve a gold medal and a pat on the back for good work too—when you conquer the urge and stay in your limits. And moderating will get easier and easier.

By the Way, How Are You Doing?

Reality-check time. Are you meeting many high-risk drinking challenges? Beating the urge with the lifestyle, behavioral, cognitive, and motivational strategies and techniques you've learned so far? Staying within daily and weekly drink limits much of the time? Starting to feel comfortable with your healthy new drinking habits? Are others noticing your new drinking habits too? These are important questions you should ask yourself midway through the program.

Look at your progress critically. Which areas do you need to concentrate on and improve? Do you need to come up with a more passionate motivational pep talk? Perfect your programming technique and really follow through with your drinking plan of action? Add more and more Drink/Link Behavior Management Skills to your repertoire every week? Keep the Basics in mind?

Which are your strongest areas? And which ones need work?

Remember, you're guaranteed reduced alcohol consumption, better drinking habits, and preventing alcoholism—if you follow the program 100 percent. So get busy and make the necessary adjustments to make your safe-drinking goal.

Remind Yourself Changing Drinking Behavior Is a Gradual Process

Shakespeare wrote, "To climb steep hills requires slow pace at first." Changing your drinking behavior—your "steep hill"—"requires slow pace" too.

And learning to moderate is like learning to walk. First you hold your head up. Then you're standing up in your crib. Next you're crawling. Soon you're lunging from chair to chair. And the next thing you know, you're walking!

Improving your drinking habits and reducing alcohol consumption over the long term involves the same learning process. First you define what safe drinking is and learn the Basics. Then you pace yourself and tune in to your drinking cues and how to beat the urge. You learn how to handle social drinking, determine your drinking personality, and find permanent solutions to underlying causes encouraging your problem drinking. And you profit from drinking mistakes. Finally, you accomplish your healthy-drinking goal! You're walking!

You've learned a lot so far. And there's more to come. Sticking with the program through thick and thin—the ups and downs of change—will make you a winner at moderation and life!

During the Week

Explore the world of natural highs. Brainstorm goodies that reinforce your brand-new drinking habits. And think of the fun you'll have when you've made the moderation grade and are lounging on the beach in Hawaii or throwing a safe-drinking bash to honor yourself!

Keep up your Drinking Diary and Drink Graph. And complete the "Natural High" Teaser midweek.

Your "vacation" this week will give you the blast of energy you need to complete the program. So kick back and enjoy!

Week Four: "Natural High" Teaser

What alcohol-free fun do you have planned—instead of drinking? List at least five activities.

What rewards do you have planned when you beat the urge, practice behavior management skills, and stay within your drink limits? List at least five.

What are the easiest aspects of your behavior change?

Which ones need more work?

What drinking challenges do you have coming up in the next week?

How will you handle them? Describe your drinking plans of action.

6

WEEK FIVE: Master the Art of Social Drinking

It's been said that dignity is the one thing that can't be preserved in alcohol.

If you sacrifice your dignity and drink too much at parties, it's time you sat up and took notice. You're about to master the art of social drinking.

Here are ten simple social drinking "ground rules" designed to help you stay in control and within your drink limit.

Treasure them and you'll never worry about your dignity or drinking in public again!

Ground Rule No. 1: Know Dangerous Drinking Cues Inside Out

Maybe you feel shy and uncomfortable trying to make small talk, and alcohol loosens you up. Maybe you think you're more charming. Or you feel more confident. Alcohol—in small doses—is an effective social lubricant.

Or drinking thinking tells you you deserve a "good time."

Or you're stressed-out and this is a great opportunity to blow off steam.

Maybe overdrinking and getting drunk is the norm for you and your hard-drinking pals—and you feel pressured into a drinking contest. Or you think a celebration just isn't a celebration unless you drink and drink and drink.

What dangerous drinking cues get you in trouble at parties? What does your drinking thinking sound like when you're facing a high-risk social drinking event? Check out your Drinking Diary for hot leads.

Knowing exactly what variables push your drinking buttons at parties will defuse their power and may give you the insight and drive you need to change them or your reaction to them.

Ground Rule No. 2: Say What You Mean and Mean What You Say

"In my pre-Drink/Link days, I'd never say no to anyone wanting to fill my glass. I was a pushover. And I paid for it with a hangover the next day. Now that I've got this effective communication thing down—telling my host or waiter when to stop—I feel a lot better physically and mentally the next day," said Sue, a San Francisco socialite.

Communicating clearly and directly to the server will eliminate any confusion and the chance you may go overboard. So let your server know when you're ready to slow down or stop in polite but certain terms.

Effective communication fundamentals? Determine your needs: the need to nurse your drink—and stick to the one-drink, one-hour Basic; the need to stay within your drink limits—and the three-drinks-max Basic. Express your needs to your server. And thank them for honoring your request.

What if you're faced with a server who always has a bottle in their hand, thinking that getting their guests drunk makes for a good host and successful party? Avoid falling into this trap by simply covering your drink with your hand to indicate you're fine.

If you're sitting at a table, push your glass away or put a napkin over it, sending the message that you're satisfied and don't need more alcohol. Ask for water or a nonalcoholic drink instead.

Communicating clearly—verbally or nonverbally—to your server is your responsibility, just like preplanning and following through with your plan.

Ground Rule No. 3: Perfect the Art of the Polite Refusal

Knowing how to say no without stepping on anyone's toes is another trick to sensible social drinking. And perfecting the art of the polite and positive refusal will put the issue of continued drinking to rest—for everyone.

When pressed to drink more, offer a polite refusal. Maybe you're driving and are allowed only one or two drinks. Or you're watching your weight—and we all know how fattening alcohol is. Or you're on a moderation program and want to reduce your alcohol consumption— fascinating cocktail conversation. Or you have a big day tomorrow and don't want to wake up with a hangover.

Come equipped with a polite refusal guaranteed to get you off the hook—and in control.

Rehearse all the polite refusals you feel comfortable with in your head first. Or role-play with a Drink/Link buddy. Then put them to work when faced with a social drinking challenge.

Ground Rule No. 4: Don't Drink Before or After a Social Drinking Occasion

Makes sense, doesn't it? No drinking before or after partying?

Unfortunately, many of us suffer from drinking thinking that tells us to have a drink or two before we even reach the party, so that we'll feel relaxed and talkative by the time we get there.

Harry was a prime example. He took to the program, but found social drinking an ordeal. Collecting fine wine was his hobby, and he attended wine tastings a couple of times a week and sometimes overdrank.

Then he got wise to two facts. His Drinking Diary indicated he'd always have a couple of glasses of wine before attending a drinking function. And if he cut drinking before a wine tasting, he'd still enjoy the party and stay within his limits.

"Once I realized that I didn't *need* to have a couple of glasses before I went to a party—an old habit I developed years ago to loosen me up—I mastered my high-risk wine tastings." So long to Harry's overdrinking.

Not drinking before you attend a drinking function could spell success for you too and keep you in charge—like Harry.

Same goes for drinking once the party's over. Get out of the habit of continuing to celebrate and drink. Another simple tip to keeping alcohol consumption down and feeling good the next day.

It doesn't take a rocket scientist to figure out you'll be well on your way to getting drunk if you allow yourself to drink before and after a social occasion, in addition to the drinks you'll have at the party. Wise up—and you'll stay in control.

Ground Rule No. 5: Program! Program! Program!

Remember the six steps involved in programming yourself for high-risk drinking scenes? Been practicing them diligently? If you have, you're becoming an old pro at preplanning and following through with your brand-new drinking habits.

If not, it's time to brush up on your programming skills, because preplanning—before a drop of alcohol even touches your lips at a social event—may be the most important ground rule of all.

You're no longer leaving your drinking to chance as you did before you started the program. You've charted a safe-drinking course and will enjoy yourself more than ever now that drinking controls are in place.

Take your programming break a couple of hours before the event and sit quietly with eyes closed if possible. Imagine how you'll think and feel when you arrive. And visualize the setting—the people, places, circumstances.

Anticipate the action—what the conversation will sound like and what liquor and food will be served.

Now preplan your drinking behavior. How long will you drink? Remember the Basics—three hours max. How many drinks will you have? Three drinks max.

Which behavior management skills will help you observe the Basics and stay within your daily drink limits? Get creative with all the skills you've learned so far and plug them in where needed.

Perhaps you'll start with a nonalcoholic beverage—delaying that first alcoholic drink by at least half an hour. And you'll snack too—taking the edge off your appetite and eliminating the possibility the alcohol will go to your head and that you'll exceed .06 BAC and lose control. If it's a long party, you'll alternate with nonalcoholic drinks—since you know you're only allowed three drinking hours.

If it's a business function, zero in on potential customers and clients and make intelligent conversation. You could turn this into a money-making event if you keep your wits about you and impress them. Keeping your mind on business—not drinking—is a clever strategy to take your mind off alcohol.

If it's a purely social occasion, discuss topics that are important to you to distract yourself and help you focus on people and fun—not drinking.

Maintain your "charm school" drinking manners, too, by sipping—not gulping—and putting your drink down between sips. Pacing yourself with these simple behavioral tips could keep you sane.

Is drinking thinking getting between you and safe social drinking? Hopefully you've already given a lot of thought to how you rationalize heavy drinking before you hit a social event. And you've poked holes in the logic of those rationalizations.

If the going gets tough and drinking thinking really kicks in, you'll direct it. Replace negative drinking thinking with positive inner conversation. Remember other accomplishments that required a lot more self-control than just passing up that next drink. Managing the urge and slowing down or stopping drinking is easy compared to working your way through college!

A quick motivational pep talk could also turn the tide for you. You don't want to cross the line to alcoholism, do you?

Get the picture and a practical drinking plan of action? Tailor it to your needs and the event. Include all of the lifestyle, behavioral, cognitive, and motivational strategies and techniques you've learned that might be helpful so you can beat the urge. Rehearse the plan in your head. Then follow through!

By the time you reach your high-risk drinking party, you should feel confident and comfortable with your preplanned behavior, leaving nothing to chance and staying within your limits—painlessly.

Ground Rule No. 6: Adopt an "I Don't Need Alcohol" Attitude

Nick was a successful client in the program and had dealt with other substance abuse issues too, like overeating. He'd tried lots of diets to keep his weight down, but it wasn't until he changed his attitude about food that he successfully kept the weight off.

He adopted an "I don't need food" attitude. Instead of obsessing about what he was going to eat throughout the day, he put food in its proper perspective.

Eating nutritious, low-fat, well-prepared food was a treat and a means to an end to stay fit and feel good—a healthy attitude about food. Food was not the be-all and end-all. And mentally focusing on it all day long was not a healthy attitude.

So when he caught himself dwelling on everything that was on the menu for the day, he dismissed it. He told himself that food was not his life and that he didn't need food to make him happy.

He put food and eating in the proper perspective, lost weight, and kept it off.

He did the same with drinking and alcohol. And succeeded in moderating and staying within his drink limits—for the long term.

You can do the same with alcohol too. When you catch yourself obsessing about when and where you'll have your first drink of the day, forget it! Drinking and alcohol are simply not that important in the overall scheme of things. And letting them rule your life can only get you in trouble.

An attitude adjustment about alcohol—putting it in its proper perspective—could loosen the grip of the urge, and you'll drink less. Think about it!

Ground Rule No. 7: Leave a Little—and Show Alcohol Who's Boss

You've finished a great meal at a fine restaurant. It's time for dessert and coffee. But your drink is half finished. You don't really want more alcohol, but you feel obligated to finish it. Waste not, want not.

Feeling you have to finish every drink—whether you want it or not—is risky. It could put you over the edge—past .06 BAC and out of control.

Get rid of this notion. Now! You're under no obligation to drink to the last drop. And leaving a drink—even if there's some left—shows who's boss. You are!

And it shows how big and strong your self-control "muscles" are getting. Try it!

Ground Rule No. 8: Think of the Morning After

Just think about what a fool you made of yourself at the last drinking party, when you threw caution to the wind, went hog-wild, and got drunk. How embarrassing!

That thought might just keep you in line and on track, observing the Basics and practicing your behavior management skills.

Remember the last time you blew a drinking party? Or did you pass out or black out and hear about your antics the next day?

Reminding yourself how embarrassed you were by your out-of-control behavior and the whopping hangover you had the next day might dampen your urge and deter heavy drinking the next time around.

So watch it. Your reputation is at stake!

Ground Rule No. 9: Get a Grip!

Sue would go 'round and 'round with herself in social drinking situations. She would get so bogged down with all the inner conversation encouraging or discouraging more drinking, she'd give up—and drink.

When she discovered the get-a-grip ground rule, she simplified her life and stayed within her limits when she partied. Getting a grip might work for you too.

Instead of letting drinking thinking get the best of you and endlessly tossing around the pros and cons of continued drinking—like Sue—now you can take the lead.

Look at how silly you're being—wasting so much time and energy trying to rationalize another drink. Save all of the excuses and energy and just say no to the next drink. So simple!

You're not a slave to alcohol and now you can prove it!

Ground Rule No. 10: Make Wise Drinking Choices

Your life is filled with choices—including choices about your drinking behavior.

You can settle for the bad habits you picked up from your parents or continue to drink in response to emotions and stress, or you can connect with Drink/Link and learn healthy drinking habits.

You can choose to observe the Drink/Link Basics or ignore them. You can practice programming, be prepared and feel confident with a drinking plan of action when you're confronted with a dangerous drinking party, or you could enter cold—leaving your drinking to chance as you always have.

You can choose to practice all of the Drink/Link Behavior Management Skills you've learned and decide which ones work best for you. Or you can practice only your favorites—limiting your behavior management repertoire.

Your life is filled with choices, and now you have safe drinking choices to make too. It's up to you—like everything else in life—to make these choices.

Do you choose to reduce your alcohol consumption or continue in your same old problem-drinking pattern?

From Disaster to Triumph Over Social Drinking—Judy's Story

Judy had dealt with problem social drinking ever since she was a teenager. Her first experiences with alcohol were with high school friends—and they'd always binge. She never really knew how to deal with the problem and often just avoided drinking altogether in social settings.

"It seems like every time I start enjoying myself at a party or with friends, I'd lose track of my drinking. I'd get lost in conversation and just keep drinking—and forget about anything else.

"Before I knew it, I'd be intoxicated. I couldn't drive. And I'd either sleep on a friend's couch or someone would have to drive me home. Was I ever embarrassed the next day! I hate to be known as someone who can't hold her liquor!"

Judy took the program to heart and worked hard on high-risk social drinking. Six weeks into the program, she was faced with a major challenge.

Old drinking friends were celebrating their twentieth wedding anniversary, and they were having a big bash. She knew she'd be tempted to overdrink. So she devised her drinking game plan.

The morning of the party, she sat quietly and thought about her reasons for wanting to moderate. Her reputation and self-esteem were at stake. Just thinking about how ashamed she felt when she "lost it" could provide the drive she needed to behave herself.

Besides, she had promised herself a new wardrobe if she could meet her safe-drinking goal—especially in social scenes.

Good start! Motivational pep talk and rewards for meeting this intimidating challenge!

She reviewed the Basics and the behavior management skills. Then she programmed herself for the event.

She anticipated the circumstances of the party. It was an afternoon affair—starting at two. There were going to be over one hundred people there—lots of friends who were drinkers too.

She felt comfortable with the company but anxious about her drinking. So she decided to take a run in the morning to blow off steam—and anxiety—that might get her in trouble.

A nonalcoholic drink would be her first drink. And she'd snack, so that she wouldn't get too high too fast on the first alcoholic drink.

She'd watch the clock, nursing her drink to stay within her one-per-hour limit. And she'd set a three-drink limit over at least three hours. Remember the Basics?

Instead of mindlessly drinking, she was going to make a point of tuning in to the effects of the alcohol—helping her to stay under her .06 BAC—which was four drinks over three hours for a woman of her weight.

She was prepared to direct her drinking thinking too and was full of positive inner conversation and affirmations. She told herself that if she took charge of every other aspect of her life, why not drinking?

Drinking thinking telling her to "go ahead, have a good time" was absurd, she thought. She rationalized she deserved a "good time" because she worked so hard and was so conscientious in every other respect. She does deserve a good time—but without getting drunk!

She followed her drinking game plan 100 percent. Even her friends noticed a difference, compared to her old social drinking bouts. She stuck to her limits and met her safe-drinking goal.

The party was a social drinking coup for her! But best of all, her self-esteem and confidence soared. She felt good about herself and her ability to beat the urge and manage social drinking in the future. She took control this time—and she could the next time too.

During the Week

Have you been focusing on your pot of gold at the end of the rainbow—a healthier, happier life—with your daily motivational pep talk? Keeping your Drinking Diary and Drink Graph current? Programming and observing your new social drinking ground rules when challenged with dangerous drinking parties? Rewarding yourself for a job well done when you stay within your limits? Exploring natural highs too? Self-confidence and self-control on the upswing?

Complete the "Master Social Drinking" Teaser midweek and set your sights on safe-drinking success.

Week Five: "Master Social Drinking" Teaser

When was the last time you blew a social drinking party? Describe the internal and external variables that triggered your urge and left you in your cups.

How would you handle that same social drinking disaster today? Describe your drinking plan of action—and all the behavior management skills you've learned so far—that would have made it a drinking success for you rather than a failure.

What drinking challenges do you have coming up in the week ahead?

How will you handle them? Describe your drinking plans of action.

7

WEEK SIX: What Drives You to Drink? Fix It!

Has drinking every night become a mindless habit? Do emotions push your drinking buttons? Has your daily schedule made drinking a necessity—a "quick fix"—because you don't have the time or energy to enjoy other types of relaxation? Do you go off the deep end—and get drunk—when you party?

You'll have to learn healthy ways to handle the issues that drive you to drink and promote your particular problem-drinking "personality" if you're going to moderate permanently.

And that's just what you'll do this week. You're going to get the big picture now by taking a closer, deeper look at your problem-drinking personality, tuning in to the mentality behind it, analyzing your drinking cycle, and learning better ways to cope with the issues promoting your particular drinking style to break your cycle and fix your problem-drinking personality.

We'll make it easy for you using the 1-2-3 method to help you sort it out.

Your goals this week? Making healthy lifestyle and attitude adjustments to manage the issues that drive you to drink, breaking your drinking cycle, and fixing your drinking personality in order to stay within safe drinking limits forever.

What's Your Dominant Drinking Personality?

You've accumulated tons of information about your drinking style and the internal and external variables that trip your drinking urge—if you've been faithful to your Drinking Diary.

Now put all those bits and pieces together and get an overall picture of your drinking personality.

The four most common drinking personalities? Habitual drinking—automatically drinking at the same time or place every day for no good reason. Emotional drinking— self-medicating with alcohol when faced with good or bad feelings. Stress-related drinking—drinking in response to the ups and downs of everyday living. And binge drinking— going off the deep end and getting drunk most of the time once you start drinking.

You probably don't fit neatly into only one category. In fact, most of us can identify with a couple of different drinking personalities. Maybe habitual and stress-related drinking ring a bell for you. Or you can really relate to emotional and binge drinking.

You're not abnormal if you connect with a couple of different styles. You may have multiple drinking personalities!

Remember, knowledge is power, and the more insight you have into your drinking style—knowing your drinking cycle and mentality inside out and how to interrupt it—the more power you'll have over it and the greater your chances of conquering it.

What drinking personalities can you identify with, according to your Drinking Diary? And what's your dominant one?

Now Kiss Your Problem-Drinking
Personality Goodbye

You've got to go out of your way and take an active role in modifying your behavior if you're going to break your drinking cycle and kiss your problem-drinking personality goodbye.

How are you going to do it? You're going to practice the old 1-2-3 technique. First, you'll look at your drinking cycle—the thought and action stages of it. Second, you'll tune in to the mentality behind it. And third, you'll short-circuit the cycle—in the thought or action stages—with Drink/Link Behavior Management Skills, breaking your drinking cycle and changing your behavior as a result.

Some of these skills may sound familiar to you. And some are brand-new. Each is designed to interrupt your particular drinking style and make way for your healthy new drinking cycle and personality.

You've already learned to program a drinking plan of action for future drinking occasions to beat the urge.

Now you're programming yourself with a long-term plan of action to resolve the issues behind your problem-drinking personality.

Fix Your Problem-Drinking Personality
Easy as 1-2-3!

1. Visualize your problem drinking cycle.

2. Reflect on the mentality behind it.

3. Break your drinking cycle in the thinking
and action stages of it and fix
your problem-drinking personality!

You'll realize your safe-drinking goal forever, nipping the causes in the bud. Easy as 1-2-3!

Are You a Slave to a Drinking Habit?

What's a habit? It's an activity you perform without even thinking.

Do you automatically head for the liquor cabinet or fridge and start drinking when you get home from work? Is wine with lunch a habit? Drinking with certain friends a given?

How many different drinking habits have you formed? Don't be discouraged—psychologists say it takes as little as three to six weeks to break a bad habit and replace it with a new one.

Imagine—practicing your healthy new drinking habits for just three weeks could be all it takes!

When Sam went into real estate, wining and dining clients was expected. He started drinking at lunch and after work with clients and collegues everyday.

This ritual took its toll. After a couple of years, a day without alcohol was inconceivable to him. His drinking habit had evolved into a heavy-drinking problem.

Your drinking habit may have evolved as a result of a change in routine too—like Sam—or in response to an event or emotion.

Lonnie started drinking when she was nursing her mother through a painful illness. She started having a glass of wine before she went to the hospital and in the evenings to feel better. And she continued the same drinking pattern—even after her mom recovered.

She realized her drinking had become a habit. She was no longer drinking to comfort herself. She was drinking because it had become a daily routine, which is an excellent example of how we may start to drink in response to feelings and become chained to a drinking habit.

How did your drinking habit start? Trace it back.

Did you have a change in your daily routine—a different work or school schedule? Did you begin taking clients to lunch where drinking was expected, or socializing with drinking friends who always had a cocktail in their hand?

Or were you stressed-out over money or a relationship, leading you to drink more often? Did you soon settle into a comfortable drinking habit? And even though the money or relationship issues have long since been resolved, are you still drinking every day?

Are you drinking at the same time, place, with the same drinking buddies, or under the same circumstances, according to your Drinking Diary? You could be a slave to a drinking habit. Now you can practice the following 1-2-3 technique and end your slavery.

1. Visualize Your Habitual Drinking Cycle. The first stage of your cycle starts with a change in internal and external variables. Either you've had a change in routine or are drinking in response to emotions or stress.

Within a short time, your new drinking pattern becomes second nature to you. And you start to anticipate that drink at a certain time of day or with special drinking buddies or at certain drinking places.

That first drink or two that you've been looking forward to relaxes you—you feel better in no time. This reinforces more drinking.

Next thing you know, you've formed a habit. You expect to drink at a special time of day, with special friends, in special places.

Visualize your habitual drinking cycle. Envision the "thinking" and "acting" stages of your cycle in your head—before you slip into them.

The more aware of the habitual drinking process you are, the less vulnerable you'll be to it!

What Does Your Habitual Drinking Cycle Look Like?

1. Internal or external variables trigger your drinking urge.

2. You drink.

3. The effects of alcohol reinforce continued drinking.

4. This drinking pattern continues for at least three weeks.

5. A drinking habit is formed.

2. Reflect on Your Habitual Drinking Mentality. Habitual drinkers suffer from a "teddy bear" mentality. Instead of hugging their teddy bear for comfort and security, they embrace alcohol and drinking.

Drinking and the euphoria of alcohol become a part of your day. Alcohol is an old friend you look forward to being with every day. And you feel empty when you deviate from this routine—and miss the drinking ritual.

Just understanding the teddy bear mentality behind your habitual drinking defuses its power over your drinking behavior.

3. Break Your Habitual Drinking Cycle and Fix Your Problem-Drinking Personality. Replacing any thought or action in your drinking cycle that promotes your particular drinking personality is your objective.

Next time the urge strikes, visualize your drinking cycle and plan on how you'll short-circuit it.

Could you stop it in the thinking stage? With a motivational pep talk, positive inner conversation or by remembering how embarrassed you felt after a heavy drinking episode? Or by inserting any other cognitive and motivational techniques you're about to learn to break the habitual drinking routine?

Or in the action stage? By participating in plenty of activities to keep you busy when the urge strikes or by having a nonalcoholic drink instead of the real thing? Or by inserting any other behavioral tips you're about to learn to interrupt the habit?

You have dozens of behavior management skills at your fingertips, and here are more—specifically designed to break the drinking habit. Plug them in, put them to work, and you'll be enjoying moderate drinking in no time—easy as 1-2-3!

Kick the Habit—Now! Perhaps the easiest way to get out of the habit is to commit to an alcohol-free period. A week? A month? Three months? It's a surefire way to break the habit—and get out of the same old drinking thinking that rationalizes automatic drinking.

Not drinking, just like drinking, can become a habit too. A healthy habit!

Prepare to feel a little "off" the first week, and make sure you've got tons of distracting activities and are full of motivational pep talk when the urge kicks in. But after that initial "off" feeling, you'll start to feel that not drinking is the norm.

Once you've beat that old habitual drinking urge—with your alcohol-free period—you'll feel even more confident in your ability to break your drinking cycle and fall into a new safe-drinking habit.

Out of Sight, Out of Mind Keeping alcohol out of the house is another surefire way to break a drinking habit—especially if your home is the scene of your habitual drinking.

Limiting your drinking to social occasions outside the house will interrupt your drinking routine and produce the desired effect—no more habitual drinking!

Hug Your Teddy Bear—Not the Bottle Next time you're suffering from a teddy bear mentality—craving the comfort and security of your drinking routine—stop!

Hug your teddy bear instead. Treat yourself to comfort food. Love the cat. Give your kids or plants a little extra attention. Anything that can give you that warm, fuzzy feeling you're craving—without alcohol.

Alcohol is not comfort food. And a drinking habit is not a harmless teddy bear. So keep your nonalcoholic comforts close at hand when the desire to drink hits.

Get Busy When the Urge Strikes Distracting yourself while fighting knee-jerk drinking is the number one way of changing your drinking ways. Programming and pre-planning—with distracting activities—to fill the times when you would start drinking is elementary to breaking the habit.

Remember, if you can distract yourself for five or ten minutes, the urge may pass or you may be able to delay that first drink—breaking your habit in the action stage.

You've got your "101 Distractions to Keep You From Drinking" list (see chapter 3) and you should have made up ten of your own.

Look at your schedule and plug in a nondrinking activity for ritual drinking times for the next three weeks, the minimum time period to break a bad habit and form a new one.

You'll be amazed at how productive you can be when you fill your time with constructive activities—not destructive drinking!

Get Your Feelings Off Your Chest When you're feeling a strong desire to slip into your drinking habit, sit down and write about your drinking thinking and feelings wrapped around it.

Feeling deprived because you're denying yourself that drink? Does it feel unnatural when you replace that first cocktail with a diet soda? Are you depressed at the thought of giving up that glass of wine with lunch? Think it's the one and only treat you allow yourself for the day in this cold, cruel world? Does it beat feeling lonely or bored?

Get it off your chest. Seeing through your drinking thinking and expressing these feelings will enable you to deal with the "loss" of the drinking habit and the "profit" of a healthy new one.

Talk to a Buddy Are you lucky enough to have a trusted, kind friend willing to listen to you blow off steam about breaking a drinking habit? Or a buddy who is also practicing the program and shooting for a safe-drinking goal?

If so, take advantage of the relationship. Call him up at the time you'd normally settle into your drinking routine. Discuss your feelings about drinking. Or the latest news. Invite him to dinner or a movie. Anything—as long as it keeps you from engaging in that old problem-drinking pattern.

Nobody said it was going to be easy to break a deeply ingrained habit. You're challenging the status quo, bucking your drinking system! Sharing the process with a trusted friend may help you through.

Give Yourself a Break—a Motivational Pep Talk Break
After you've sorted out all of the drinking thinking that
encourages your drinking habit, give yourself a break—a
positive inner conversation break.

Think of your successes in the program so far. Remind
yourself that you're taking charge of your life and alcohol.
And recall other challenges in your life that were a lot
tougher—and how you triumphed over them.

Talk yourself out of drinking and into following through
with your drinking plan of action—and breaking the habit.

Just Stop! Joe was a habitual drinker. He had a bad
habit of reaching for a beer around five P.M.—the first thing
he did when he got home from work. Nothing seemed to
work to kick this habit.

Then one day, when asked what he could possibly do to
nip this habit in the bud, he came up with a solution. Plas-
tering a big red STOP sign on the refrigerator door at
home when he felt the urge for that first beer would do the
trick.

Worked like a charm! No motivational pep talk, no
reviewing thinking and feelings, and no planned distractions. He just obeyed the STOP sign on the refrigerator
door, and that was the end of that. Plain and simple.

It might work for you too. You don't get bogged down
with self-talk and you don't have to work at plugging in
Behavior Management Skills. You just tell yourself no, and
within five or ten minutes the urge has passed and you're
well on your way to breaking a habit!

Make Intelligent Decisions   By making intelligent decisions—and putting the Behavior Management Skills to
work for you—you can take charge and kick the drinking
habit.

Making stupid decisions—and allowing yourself to continue to be a slave to an alcohol habit—will increase your
psychological and physical dependence on alcohol. And

your only option will be abstinence—unless you address your drinking habit right now!

It's the smart thing to do.

Carol, Habitual Drinker—and Success Story!

Carol was a single mom and started her own business. Busy lady! But three years after starting it, she realized she had developed a bad drinking habit.

She worked late—till at least seven-thirty every night. And she "treated" herself to a glass of wine at the end of the day.

The habit grew—she was "treating" herself to wine at the same time even when she wasn't working, and one glass of wine turned into two, three, four, and eventually the whole bottle after three years.

Unfortunately, her little treat had become a nasty habit. And alcohol and its effects had become her security blanket.

Carol tailored the Drink/Link Moderation Program to her needs and schedule. Her mornings were her "quiet" times during the day. So she took advantage of this time to give herself a motivational pep talk—about why drinking less was so important to her.

She wanted to be a better role model to her kids, who had noticed her drinking and hounded her about it. And she was health-conscious and worried that her escalating drinking problem would become alcoholism if she didn't get busy and address the problem now. Three excellent reasons why sticking with the program and reducing alcohol consumption were so important to her.

Carol was smart enough to realize that a two-week break from any drinking would give her a fresh start and a new outlook on drinking and alcohol. So she didn't drink for two weeks—before tackling the habit.

When she did start drinking again, she was well equipped with a short-term and long-term drinking plan of action to break her drinking cycle and the habit.

She visualized her habitual drinking cycle and programmed herself for the day. She anticipated returning home after work and wanting to drink wine—including all of the drinking thinking and feelings surrounding her desire to drink.

And she preplanned her behavior for the evening. She reminded herself of the Basics—three drinks over three hours allowed for drinking days. Instead of immediately going for the wine, she decided to start with a nonalcoholic drink—replacing alcohol with iced tea in the "action" stage of her drinking cycle. She set a two-drink limit in advance—one glass of wine before dinner and one with her meal.

She would focus on her kids—they would be her teddy bears, not alcohol. And she would concentrate on dinner.

After dinner she'd have a couple of mints, keeping her busy and signaling her drinking was done to break the thinking and action stages of her drinking cycle.

Watching the clock and observing the one-drink, one-hour Basic and alternating with iced tea after the first glass of wine were also on her agenda.

After dinner she knew she'd be exhausted but would still want another glass of wine—her old habit.

Instead of giving in to the urge, she would "treat" herself to some positive inner conversation—and short-circuit the thinking stage of her cycle. She had started and developed a successful business on her own in only three years. She could certainly break a drinking habit!

Then she reviewed her drinking thinking. She knew she'd try to dream up a good excuse to keep drinking—for example, that another glass of wine would ensure a good night's rest. She was prepared for the drinking thinking trap, but wouldn't fall into it.

She decided to "get a grip" and just stop for the evening and go to bed—an appropriate response to being tired—instead of indulging in more drinking.

Then she rehearsed her drinking plan in her head. And she'd stick to it—interrupting her habitual drinking pattern. She was ready to challenge habitual drinking that day.

With her careful programming, practicing the old 1-2-3 technique, and looking at long-term solutions, she cut her drinking in half! From six glasses of wine every night to two or three on her five drinking days per week.

Best of all, according to Carol, she no longer felt chained to an alcohol habit. A real success story for Carol—and you too if you follow the program the way she did.

Carol broke her drinking cycle and fixed her habitual drinking personality in the process. She looks forward to lasting success—now that she's gotten to the core of the problem.

Are You a Prisoner of Emotional Drinking?

You've just had a tiff with your mate. Or you discover you didn't get that promotion at work you'd been hoping for. You've met the person of your dreams and feel on top of the world. The car needs an overhaul and your credit cards are maxed out. The big deal with the huge commission has gone through and you're ecstatic. Or you're feeling guilty about falling off the moderation program last night and drinking over your limit.

What is your response to these negative emotions or states of mind (anger, frustration, anxiety, or depression) or positive emotions (joy and self-confidence)? Drinking!

Within ten or fifteen minutes, alcohol can enhance an emotional high or put out an emotional "fire"—making the world a nicer place. It can take the edge off loneliness or depression and turn a humdrum evening into a party.

It's cheap, legal, and socially acceptable. No wonder so many of us rely upon it for its calming and euphoric properties.

Is drinking an emotional "reaction" for you? When you're dealing with positive or negative emotions, do you "medicate" with alcohol to enhance or soothe those feelings?

If you turn to alcohol to cope with your feelings, you're suffering from emotional drinking. And you're drinking inappropriately.

How many entries in your Drinking Diary indicate you're drinking in response to feelings or a state of mind? How many times have you turned to alcohol because you were feeling blue, lonely, angry, frustrated, anxious, or tense? And how many times did you start drinking or overdrink because you felt confident, successful, happy, or in love?

Don't get upset about emotional drinking—and start drinking. Manage it—1-2-3!

1. Visualize Your Emotional Drinking Cycle. Emotional drinking starts with a feeling or state of mind—positive or negative.

What Does Your Emotional Drinking Cycle Look Like?

1. Internal variables—positive or negative emotions or states of mind—trigger your urge.

2. You anticipate the effects of alcohol.

3. You drink.

4. Alcohol soothes or enhances those feelings reinforcing drinking.

5. You continue to drink.

You anticipate the effects of alcohol—soothing the pain or enchancing the pleasure. You drink. It works! You're feeling better or really celebrating in no time! It works so well, drinking is reinforced—you continue to drink and drink too much. And you've fallen into the emotional drinking trap.

Visualize your emotional drinking cycle before you slip into it. And you may break the cycle!

2. Reflect on Your Emotional Drinking Mentality. Emotional drinking is reactive drinking. Alcohol helps you cope with feelings. And drinking is the result.

Alcohol is not "medicine" to help you deal with feelings. And drinking is an unhealthy reaction to emotions and an inappropriate use of alcohol.

Rid yourself of this emotional drinking mentality and you'll take a giant step to ridding yourself of emotional drinking.

3. Break Your Emotional Drinking Cycle. Replacing any thought or action in your drinking cycle that leads you to problem drinking is your objective.

Next time the urge strikes, visualize your drinking cycle. And plan on how you'll short-circuit it.

In the thinking stages, draw on any and all cognitive and motivational strategies and techniques you've learned so far and the ones you're about to learn to alter your drinking cycle.

In the action stages, draw on any and all behavioral and lifestyle strategies and techniques you've already learned and new ones you're about to learn.

Finding healthy ways to deal with emotions, rather than unhealthy ways—like drinking—will ensure your sensible new drinking habits forever. Practice them!

Get in Touch With Your Feelings   The first step to conquering emotional drinking is acknowledging the feelings whetting your appetite for alcohol.

What negative high-risk emotions or states of mind push your drinking buttons? Loneliness? Depression? Anger?

Anxiety? Frustration? Nervousness? Helplessness? Pressure? Boredom? Hurt? Indifference? Hopelessness? Sadness? Isolation? Low self-esteem?

What positive high-risk feelings push your drinking buttons?

Overconfidence? Ambition? High self-esteem? Love? Sex? Celebration? Friendship? Self-indulgence?

Which feelings or states of mind affect you and your drinking behavior? Check out your Drinking Diary.

Recognize them and how they push you over the drinking edge, and they'll be less likely to influence you.

Learn Healthy Ways to Cope With Feelings What are some healthy responses to feelings? Talk about them. Write about them. Resolve them. Resign yourself to them. Laugh at them.

Exercising. Deep breathing. Meditating. Cleaning the house. Playing with the kids. Loving your puppy. Acknowledging your feelings. Turning cartwheels.

Anything as long as you don't resort to alcohol to deal with them.

Next time around, when you're faced with emotional drinking cues triggering your urge and setting off your emotional drinking cycle, concentrate on healthy responses. Without alcohol.

Resolve the Issues Behind Your Feelings If you can resolve the issues that spark the emotions and start you drinking, you're finding a permanent solution—not a temporary "quick fix" with alcohol.

First, define the problem or the circumstances that give rise to your feelings. Be specific.

Then record all of your potential responses to the situation. Get creative!

Sleep on the solutions. And decide which course of action would resolve or improve the situation.

Go for it! Put your plan to work. Give it time and see the results.

If it works—and you're no longer suffering from the effects of the issue or a drinking reaction—great!

But if you're not satisfied with the results, go on to the next best solution—and keep working on it.

When you've exhausted your options, think about professional counseling.

The sooner you resolve the issues behind emotional drinking, the sooner you'll break the cycle and meet your safe-drinking goal for the long term.

Rational and Realistic—Prescription for Feelings and Drinking Looking at your feelings in a different light might eliminate or limit your emotional response to them—and decrease your desire for alcohol.

Emotions are physical and psychological reactions to people and events. Often we overreact to them. Our emotional responses are not rational or realistic.

Putting a lid on emotional extremes and putting feelings in perspective increases your objectivity and enables you to come up with sensible solutions to emotional issues. Then you are no longer emotionally bound to them. So stay cool!

And if you're drinking to put out the fires of negative emotions, you'll be disappointed. Sure, the first drink or two may take the emotional edge off, but more alcohol just exacerbates your feelings. It fires you up—instead of settling you down!

Rational and realistic—a good prescription for curbing emotional drinking.

Try a "Talking Cure"—and Eliminate the Emotional Drinking Need If you're having a tough time keeping cool and are unable to arrive at sensible solutions to what's bugging you, keep professional counseling open as an option.

Short-term counseling—a "talking cure"—might be just what the doctor ordered. You may be able to get your feelings off your chest and resolve the issues shaking you up in record time.

The result? A happier, healthier, moderate-drinking individual sooner than you think—a person who is no longer chewing on an emotionally charged issue like a dog with a bone!

Remember the Mornings After Your Emotional Drinking? Just knowing how bad you feel about yourself after a bout of unhealthy emotional drinking is a terrific deterrent to it.

Picture yourself waking up the next day with an emotional and physical hangover, feeling guilty and depressed over your drinking, and still dealing with the unpleasant feelings that triggered it. You've fallen into the emotional drinking trap again!

Have you forgotten? You have choices—all the behavior management skills you can practice to short-circuit emotional drinking. No more guilt, shame, or overdrinking!

Next time you're facing high-risk feelings, think about the outcome of drowning your sorrows in alcohol. It gets you nowhere!

Shane Developed Emotional Drinking—and Conquered It!

Shane was the perfect example of an emotional drinker. He had just broken up with his girlfriend of five years and was devastated. Drinking was his reaction to this upset.

Shane was smart enough to realize that he didn't want a drinking problem—in addition to all of the other problems he was having—and enrolled in the program.

Lifestyle changes and the moderation program were the answers to Shane's emotional drinking problem. And he programmed short-term and long-term soltuions to his drinking behavior and emotional drinking cycle to stay out of trouble.

Staying busy was an important aspect of his drinking game plan. He joined a gym and made plans every week for at least two social activities—for example, dancing or going out to dinner or the movies with friends. Filling his time and enjoying the company of others—instead of sitting home alone, feeling blue and wallowing in self-pity—seemed like a logical first step.

And he put the program to work for him. His motivational pep talk included convincing himself that he would lead a rich and full life once he got over this "hump." He focused on other important goals in his life too—like starting his own business and buying a house. Focusing on these goals gave him the boost he needed to stick to his drinking plan of action.

Next, he programmed himself and applied the 1-2-3 technique—especially to those high-risk occasions when he was tempted to slip into emotional drinking.

He seemed most vulnerable to them after work when he was tired and when he had nothing to do—when he was alone and bored. He decided to commit to working out at the gym at least two nights a week. It kept him busy, exercise made him feel better, and he was making new friends with a nondrinking activity!

On the nights he was home, he planned on having two beers max. And instead of medicating his feelings with alcohol, he was going to acknowledge them. He'd call a friend or write about his feelings instead of burying them.

Recognizing his feelings was an important part of his drinking plan. Breaking the emotional drinking cycle at the thinking stage worked for him.

And he'd practice the simple behavioral suggestions too—alternating, delaying, distracting, sipping—all helping him to stay within his one-drink, one-hour Basic. Replacing healthy drinking behaviors at the action stage of his cycle worked too!

A well-balanced meal and a good night's rest were also on the agenda. In addition to taking good care of himself physically, emotionally, and socially, he decided to take a local community college course in creative writing—something he'd always wanted to do.

If he was really feeling blue, he would talk to a licensed counselor to help him through the tough times. Talking about his feelings and the issues behind them would decrease his appetite for alcohol.

Shane put his drinking plan in action. He felt better, his social life perked up, and he was drinking a lot less.

A detailed short-term and long-term drinking plan of action helped him stay within his safe-drinking limits.

Shane developed a healthy new drinking personality and lifestyle—and broke his emotional drinking cycle. You can too.

Are You a Victim of Stress-Related Drinking?

"I must get out of these wet clothes and into a dry martini," Alexander Woollcott said, describing the comfort of alcohol after a rough day. And a good example of stress-related drinking thinking.

Ken was a high-powered executive who dealt with extreme stress and the need to get into that dry martini each day after work. He put together million-dollar deals for celebrity clients. He paid little attention to any other aspect of his life—except the cocktail hour.

At seven-thirty or eight every night—usually when his work day ended—he gave himself permission to start drinking.

Drinking was the only stress-reducing activity he'd known for years. It was so fast and efficient. After two martinis the problems of the day simply disappeared.

Over the last two years, though, he was drinking more and more. And that concerned him. Hangovers impaired his job performance. Besides, he just couldn't see himself as a "hit-bottom" alcoholic.

That's when he decided to do something about it and enrolled in the moderation program.

Stress is a physical or psychological tension that is produced in response to a person, event, or set of circumstances.

Physical symptoms of stress include headaches, indigestion, irregular heartbeat, insomnia, back pain, muscle tension, and stomachaches.

Psychological symptoms include nervousness, anxiety, becoming easily upset, and feeling unhappy for no apparent reason. Crying at the drop of a hat, an inability to concentrate or make decisions, worrying all the time, and a lack of creativity and sense of humor may also indicate you're suffering from stress.

And overdrinking, overeating, smoking too much, and grinding your teeth at night are all behavioral symptoms of stress.

If you're suffering from any of these symptoms, it's not surprising. Lots of folks are stressed-out from complicated, hectic lifestyles these days. The trick is to deal with it in healthy ways—not unhealthy ways like overdrinking.

1. Visualize Your Stress-Related Drinking Cycle. First, you're presented with a person, event, or set of circumstances which produce physical or psychological tension—stress.

Maybe it's been a hectic day—from five in the morning to ten at night. Or you feel pressured—like Ken—in a working situation where there is a lot at stake. Or your income is not keeping up with your bills.

Whatever your stressor—the issue producing the stress— you feel pressured and tense. That's the next stage of your stress-related drinking cycle.

Then you think of the fast way out—alcohol. You anticipate how relaxed you'll feel with that first drink. You're looking forward to it—and can feel the tension draining away with it.

Relaxation and fun replace the stress with that first drink or two. And continued drinking is reinforced. You feel so good after those first couple of drinks, why stop or slow down? So you continue to drink.

The next day you realize that the more-is-better drinking thinking does not work—at least not with alcohol. You're suffering from a physical and psychological hangover. You've got a headache and an upset stomach. And you feel guilty and ashamed for drinking too much.

What Does Your Stress-Related Drinking Cycle Look Like?

1. Internal and external variables produce stress and trigger your drinking urge.

2. You look forward to the relaxing effects of alcohol.

3. You drink.

4. Stress melts away and drinking is reinforced.

5. You continue to drink.

2. Reflect on Your Stress-Related Drinking Mentality.
Stress-related drinking is "quick-fix" drinking. You're drinking to feel better fast—regardless of the consequences.

Is drinking an appropriate response to stress? Maybe one or two drinks is. But engaging in heavy drinking day in and day out is not, and will do you more harm than good.

Get the notion that alcohol is the answer to your stressed-out lifestyle out of your head! It's about time you looked into healthy, long-term solutions to reduce your stress level.

3. Break Your Stress-Related Drinking Cycle. Replacing any thought or action in your drinking cycle that leads you to problem drinking is your objective.

Next time the urge strikes, visualize your drinking cycle and how you'll short-circuit it.

In the thinking stages, you can use any or all of the cognitive and motivational strategies and techniques you've learned so far and the ones you're about to learn.

In the action stages, you can use any or all of the behavioral and lifestyle strategies and techniques you've learned so far and the ones you're about to learn.

Now translate the large repertoire of behavior management skills you've already learned and these new ones into action. And break your stress-related drinking cycle.

Kicking Your Stress-Related Drinking Cycle Starts in Your Head Changing your behavior always starts in your head. So start thinking about healthy ways to deal with stress versus unhealthy ways.

Drinking too much, eating too much, working too much—becoming addicted to any substance or activity—is not a healthy response to stress.

Lifestyle changes, exercise, practicing stress-reduction techniques, and keeping your sense of humor are healthy responses to stress.

Before you take that first drink after a rough day, be straight with yourself. This may be one way for you to relax, but it's only an easy out—and alcohol is not the answer to reducing the stress in your life permanently.

This thoughtful attitude may be your first step to overcoming a drinking reaction to stress. Think about it!

Pinpointing the Stressors in Your Life Is the Next Step
What stressors—internal and external variables—increase your stress level and your desire to drink?

Do you assume too many tasks and responsibilities at work? Is your commute a long and tedious nightmare? Do you have strained relationships with the boss and colleagues? Do you work straight through the day—no breaks or lunch?

If you can relate to any one of these situations, your work may be stressing you out and driving you to drink. What factors in your job are stressing you out?

Are your personal relationships the source of the stress? If problems with family and friends get in the way of your safe-drinking goal, it's time you sat back and took a good look at relationships and issues in relationships that drive you to drink.

Are financial problems making you crazy? You're not alone! Money—making it, spending it wisely, and saving it—is a real challenge for most of us. And alleviating money pressures could reduce your stress and your need to drink.

Raising kids is demanding too. Even more so if you're a single parent or having problems with your mate. Is juggling parenthood, career, and finances getting to you?

Or maybe you're single and can't seem to find the "right one." And you're feeling lonely and bored in the meantime and stressed over the thought of living alone the rest of your life.

Demands you place on yourself could also be triggering your desire to drink. Maybe the sacrifices you've made to buy your first house or start your own business are getting you down. Or you feel trapped in a job, but have to stick with it because you've got so many bills to pay. Or you want to change professions, but can't stand the thought of more school to help you accomplish your lofty goals.

Jot down categories for each potential stressor: work concerns, family and personal relationships, money concerns, physical health, personal fulfillment, and future concerns. And record the stressors in each category that drive you to drink.

Pinpointing exactly what's bothering you—and driving you to drink—is an important first step to changing it.

Now Make Adjustments to Take the Pressure Off   Can you put your finger on the stressors in your life? Now brainstorm on how you can "fix" them—by making simple, commonsense adjustments, so that you're no longer driven to drink.

Take work-related stress. Stop assuming more and more responsibility—and stressing out. Before you accept any more assignments, give your decision careful thought.

And take breaks! We know you're a loyal and dedicated employee, but never giving your mind or body a break doesn't increase your productivity—it decreases it. Just ten minutes midmorning and midafternoon and a half-hour lunch break *away* from work will do wonders for your mood and energy level.

If you're having problems, schedule a conference with a higher-up. Your boss wants you to be as efficient as possible, and that happens when everyone and everything is running smoothly. Together you could find a simple solution to the problem.

If you're feeling underpaid and underappreciated at work, maybe it's time you brushed up your skills with a couple of night classes. Write a new resumé, too. It may be time for a move up.

Is money an issue for you? If money—or the lack of it—is making you a nervous wreck, it's time you either tightened your belt or increased your income. You may need to increase your working hours or look for a better-paying position. And if credit card bills are the issue, perhaps consulting a professional credit counselor—an expert on how to manage your income—would be a wise investment.

Are relationships a concern? Who should make dinner, pay bills, or clean the house? Who feeds the cat, helps the kids with homework, or takes them to tennis lessons? Clearly defining your roles and expectations in a relationship is the first step to a stress-free relationship. And sharing the workload and responsibilities is the second.

If you're single and alcohol constitutes your "party for one," maybe it's time you looked into different ways of meeting others of like mind and enjoying a more active social life, taking the edge off your loneliness and appetite for alcohol.

Do you place too many demands on yourself? Go easy if you're working on a long-term goal. Treating yourself now and then—with a well-deserved vacation instead of saving every nickel and dime—will take the pressure off and make you more ambitious than ever.

You could tone down your lifestyle too. If you think you "need" more money, a bigger car, a bigger house, or more "things," you may need an attitude adjustment instead! Stop focusing on material things to make you happy. Instead, focus on things money can't buy—like fulfilling relationships, increased self-esteem, and feeling you're a good person making a real contribution to the human race. Downsizing your life could translate into downsizing your alcohol consumption.

Get the idea? Even though these stressors and the lifestyle changes seem simple, they could help you cut drinking and transform your life.

Now brainstorm solutions to your stressors and put them to work. Stress and drinking in response to it may soon be a thing of the past.

Brush Up Your Lifestyle Basics Too   So you've pinpointed your stressors and are considering simple solutions to them.

How can you feel even better? Brush up on your Lifestyle Basics!

Exercise! Plan a time in your day when you can take a walk, ride a bike, take a yoga or aerobics class, play tennis, or learn golf.

If weather doesn't permit outdoor activities, tune in to an exercise class on TV or buy a video to get you going. Your stress will evaporate with exercise—and reduce your desire for alcohol.

Plan on exercising at least three times a week.

Make a point of eating a nutritional, well-balanced diet too. Junk food and a haphazard eating schedule put nerves on edge. So does too much caffeine, sugar, and salt. So watch it!

You've heard this song before about how important sensible living habits are. The case for clean living can never be overstated.

Personalizing a wholesome lifestyle is not only a healthy way to handle stress, it also increases your feeling of well-being, decreases your appetite for alcohol, and ensures safe-drinking habits permanently.

Which Lifestyle Basics do you need to brush up on?

More No-Brainer Stress Reducers   Want more easy tips for easing stress? Simplify your life. Put things in perspective and prioritize. Think positive. Substitute fun activities for stressful ones. Talk about what's bugging you. And when all else fails, have a good laugh!

Unplug the phone and TV, shut down the computer, and disconnect the fax—just as if you were on vacation! You may be overstimulated with all these communication systems and the demands they make on you. So give yourself a break from them for a couple of hours a day. And savor the quiet time.

When you've got a million things to do in a day, don't think you have to get *everything* done. Odds are you won't. But you'll feel stressed-out at the end of the day because you didn't. Prioritize your tasks, tending to the most important ones first. If you don't get everything done, at least you'll have taken care of the most urgent matters.

Put things in perspective too. Nothing is the end of the world. With that attitude you'll sleep better at night—and drink less.

Looking on the bright side could also help. You could be a basket case if you took all of the ups and downs of your day seriously. So maintain a positive attitude—especially when the going gets tough—and you'll feel better at the end of the day.

Watch *Leave It to Beaver* or listen to Beethoven's Ninth—instead of the nightly news. Substituting pleasant activities for stressful ones is another easy way to cut your stress and your drinking.

Make a point of planning at least two fun activities during the week—a great way to blow off steam. Dinner out? A trip to the beach or ski slopes? A hike with a friend? What tickles your fancy? Do it!

Get feelings and your stressors off your chest. A heart-to-heart with a good friend, your physician or clergyman, or a professional counselor about stressors in your life could do the trick. They'll offer you a different point of view, and you'll feel better after venting your concerns.

Laughter could be the best medicine of all! Life is too short for you to get so bogged down by problems that the stress takes over and you're no longer having a good time. Looking at the funny side of a bad situation—there must be one—will drain the tension right out of you. And you'll cope with stress better.

Which "no-brainers" appeal to you? And which ones will you practice? Remember, you give them meaning by putting them to work.

Traditional Stress-Reduction Techniques Abound Maybe tried-and-true stress-reduction strategies and techniques are the answer for you. Give them serious consideration. You won't know what works for you until you try it!

Take a deep-breathing break when stress is catching up to you. Sit back, take several long, deep breaths, and relax—a "quickie" to help see you through the day and even through a drinking urge.

Or give yourself a time-out when you're ready to blow your stack or give up and start drinking. Spend five or ten minutes away from your desk or your problem and take a walk around the block, slowing your pounding heart and reducing your stress level.

What's your idea of paradise? Daydreaming about it for ten minutes and forgetting the "real" world will leave you feeling refreshed and relaxed. Are you snoozing by a stream in a quiet, cool forest? Or sunbathing on the beach of a lush tropical island? Get into it—and use your imagination to create a peaceful setting away from the stressed-out one you're trying to deal with now. Live your fantasy in your head.

Lots of people swear by meditation and yoga to cope with daily stress. Where do you start? A trip to the library could get you acquainted with all the different approaches. The next step is to pick up a book or enroll in a class teaching the one that appeals to you. You may find meditation a no-cost, convenient, and effective stress reducer that you can use whenever you need it, night or day.

Hypnosis can have a calming effect too. Hypnotic suggestion freeing one from anxiety and stress can be effective. All you have to do is find a hypnotist you're comfortable with to put you under the spell. Stress and the need to drink may vanish.

Or biofeedback could be the answer to your prayers. You know how you program yourself for future drinking occasions. You can also program your body and mind to achieve a stress-free state. Sit quietly, relax your muscles, and concentrate on slowing your breathing and lowering your heart rate. Another no-cost stress-management skill you can practice any time and any place.

Have fun exploring all the traditional relaxation and stress-reduction techniques out there. But most important, practice them!

Nontraditional Stress-Reduction Techniques Abound, Too
Ever tried an herbal remedy—like ginseng or valerian—to relieve anxiety and stress? People in other cultures have turned to herbs for centuries for whatever ails—including stress. Check it out.

Music—new age, classical, folk, nature sounds—anything to calm you down and get you to stop and smell the roses is worth a try too. Babbling brooks or dolphins communicating could get your mind off a rough day—and alcohol.

How about a massage or mud bath to melt the stress away? Sounds great—a real treat and stress buster!

Enjoying the company of a pet has been clinically proven to lower your stress level. Loving and cleaning up after a puppy or kitty will certainly take your mind off your problems.

Relaxation tapes are all the rage these days too. Guided imagery, biofeedback, hypnotic suggestions, you name it. They could be your inexpensive ticket to calming down.

Have you thought about making your home a tranquil oasis? Installing a fountain—and relaxing to water sounds? Having lots of green plants refresh you? Listening to chimes and smelling incense? Your home can become your stress-free "getaway" with a few minor adjustments.

Finally, check out the stress-management sections in your bookstore and even stress-management clinics in your area. Volumes have been written about how to relieve stress, and it's your responsibility to decide which approaches are best for you. You may see a dramatic reduction in your stress level and your alcohol consumption—if you follow up and follow through with your long-term stress-reduction plan.

Ken "Fixed" His Lifestyle—and Achieved His Safe-Drinking Goal

Remember Ken? The stressed-out, overdrinking executive who worked from seven in the morning to seven at night, six days a week? He knew he'd have to make changes in his lifestyle before he could see any difference in his drinking behavior—and he did!

His morning routine underwent some minor changes. He started work early in the morning as usual. But he cut out that third and fourth cup of coffee. Less caffeine enabled him to avoid the frayed nerves he usually had by about eleven A.M. At about that time, he took his first break of the day—something he had never done before.

Before, he would stay at his desk or in his office the entire day. Now he made a point of taking a juice break across the street—he was lucky enough to have an office right on the San Francisco waterfront. Between the juice, the blast of fresh sea air, and time out from the office, he felt better.

At noon, instead of eating at his desk, he walked a couple of blocks to a restaurant for lunch. Walking four blocks during his lunch break was really refreshing.

And he worked on an attitude adjustment about how important his work was. He told himself that losing a "big deal" was not the end of the world. If a deal fell through, it was only money! In other words, he put his life and work in perspective.

If things were not going well during the day, he would practice deep breathing and more time-outs at the office. It slowed him down and kept his stress level under control.

Toward the end of the day, he allowed himself only one more coffee, and by six P.M. he headed for home. An eleven-hour work day is more than enough for anyone.

He started to work out at a gym close to his office a couple nights a week too and paid more attention to his diet—especially eating a healthy dinner.

He also made a point of taking off one and a half, maybe even two days a week. He planned an activity that he thought he would enjoy but had never had time to fit in before his lifestyle and attitude adjustments.

Even though these changes seem simple, they were difficult for Ken at first. After all, he'd been a workaholic and couch potato for years. But once he got the hang of things, he looked forward to his exercise routine and weekend activities. And he noticed a significant reduction in stress and alcohol consumption because of these changes.

When the drinking urge struck after work, he always had a plan of action prepared. He was working out a couple of nights a week, distracting him from and delaying the same old drinking pattern. He planned on two martinis max—if he was going to drink at all. And he was full of positive inner conversation and was ready to defuse drinking thinking when challenged.

Between improving his lifestyle and programming himself with a specific drinking plan with behavior management skills he'd already learned, he made the leap from a stressed-out heavy-drinking lifestyle to a healthier, moderate-drinking lifestyle. And he felt years younger—and more productive than ever!

Isn't it about time to upgrade your lifestyle? What improvements could you make to help you reduce your stress and your appetite for alcohol?

Are You an Out-of-Control Binge Drinker?

How often do you go off the deep end, drinking a lot of alcohol in a short period of time and get drunk? Does it happen most often at a party or social function? Do you feel guilty and depressed because you make such a fool of yourself? Or do you black out—remembering nothing because you get so high so fast?

Most of us can recall at least one bingeing episode in our illustrious drinking career. Perhaps it was a drinking occasion when we threw caution to the wind and drank excessively in an uncontrolled manner. Or a drinking spree where we gave ourselves silent permission to drink as much and as long as we could until we passed out or fell asleep—even though we may not drink on a regular basis or excessively most of the time.

Karin had been worried about her bingeing behavior for seven years. In her mid-thirties, she was a devoted wife and mother, a real athlete and a personal trainer.

She rarely drank during the week. And most of the time she was fine. Often when she went out to dinner, she had no problem with just one glass of wine before dinner and one glass during dinner.

It was the exceptions—the rare occasions when she drank like there was no tomorrow—that really bothered her. Especially since there had been a history of substance abuse in her family.

Karin was the classic binge drinker. And fortunately, she had the sense to recognize it and do something about it—instead of suffering years of worry and guilt about her drinking sprees and wondering if she had inherited the same substance abuse problems her mom and uncle had.

Many of us outgrow this wild bingeing behavior. But if you notice a bingeing pattern in your Drinking Diary, it's high time you address it—1-2-3!

1. Visualize Your Binge-Drinking Cycle. Your urge to drink is the first stage of your bingeing cycle. It could be triggered by high-risk drinking variables—internal and external.

Maybe you're keeping company with hard-drinking buddies who think that drinking as much and as fast as you can is no big deal. Or you're at a social event where champagne is flowing and there is an open bar—and you feel you have to make the best of it.

Then you give yourself silent permission to drink as much and as fast as you can. Maybe you haven't enjoyed yourself like this for years. Why not drink as much as you want? Maybe you're feeling anxious and uncomfortable with the company. Why not drink more than usual—you may be more charming! Maybe you pride yourself on being very disciplined and leading a healthy lifestyle most of the time. Why shouldn't you indulge yourself now and then? Whatever your reasons—your drinking thinking—these cues lead you to bingeing behavior.

The scene is set. Liquor is flowing and you've talked yourself into going hog-wild—"rewarding" yourself for being such a conservative drinker most of the time.

What Does Your Binge-Drinking Cycle Look Like?

1. Internal and external variables trigger your drinking urge.

2. Drinking thinking takes over, giving you silent permission to go overboard.

3. You drink recklessly and heavily until you're drunk.

4. You feel ashamed and embarrassed about your out-of-control drinking.

The next day you can't remember much about the rest of the drinking party because you blacked out, or you remember all too well how out of control you were and have an ugly hangover for "treating" yourself so well!

And you feel embarrassed, guilty, and depressed about losing it and bingeing, feelings encouraging continued drinking—to numb your physical and mental hangovers!

2. Reflect on Your Binge-Drinking Mentality. You're suffering from a "splurge" mentality if you're suffering from binge drinking. Binge drinkers seem to see themselves and the world in black and white, have an all-or-nothing attitude, and pride themselves on being in total control of their lives—most of the time.

If they or the world can't be perfect—with no shades of gray confusing matters—they might as well throw in the towel, give up control, and do whatever they please—regardless of the consequences. And that includes drinking as much as they want.

Tuning in to your splurge mentality and tracing it back—seeing where you picked it up—could help you eliminate it, as well as decrease your "off-the-deep-end" behavior and your alcohol consumption.

3. Break Your Binge-Drinking Cycle. Interrupting your drinking cycle at any stage—the thinking stage or the action stage—is your goal. And you'll do this by plugging in the Drink/Link Behavior Management Skills you've already learned and new ones you're about to learn to fight bingeing.

You're in charge—of drinking thinking and actions! Do you need a motivational pep talk? Think about how proud your mate and kids would be if you broke the bingeing cycle. Try recalling the outcomes of your drinking sprees. What else can you say to yourself in the thinking stages of your bingeing cycle to break it?

Have you been paying close attention to pacing yourself and tuning in to your .06 BAC? Try focusing on dancing and conversation instead of drinking. "Get a grip"—know you're vulnerable to a bingeing urge and get yourself out of a drinking situation before it becomes too great a temptation. Talk to your mate about your desire to go all out and get drunk—instead of actually doing it. What else can you do in the action stages of your bingeing cycle to break it?

You're a sensible and intelligent human being—most of the time. Here are some more tips to help you devise a solid drinking plan of action. Follow through with it—when faced with a potential bingeing disaster.

Know Your Binge-Drinking Cues Inside Out Phil was straight as an arrow. He was a career military man and saw the world in black-and-white terms. He worked too much, and he felt stuck in an unhappy marriage.

When he saw a chance to bolt from his humdrum existence, he grabbed it. He gave up control and gave in to the urge to drink too much.

Feelings that led Phil to bingeing? He felt deprived—as many binge drinkers do. He felt overworked. He didn't enjoy a good relationship with his wife. And he felt life was a letdown in general. Feelings a lot of other binge drinkers share at one time or another.

Drinking thinking that led Phil to bingeing? Why shouldn't he take advantage of a drinking party? It's a rare opportunity to escape from life. After all, he meets all of his responsibilities—and then some—and makes a good living for his family.

Drinking and the effects of alcohol seem like a logical solution at the time. And he grants himself silent permission to drink until he is drunk.

Feelings and drinking thinking set the stage for bingeing. And when keeping company with heavy-drinking pals or challenged by a bar scene—external drinking variables triggering his bingeing urge—he gives in and loses control. He drinks mindlessly and has to get a cab home.

What are the high-risk drinking variables that give you "permission" to go hog-wild? The more you know about them, the less likely you'll fall into the bingeing trap.

"Drinking Thinking" Is Your Number One Enemy Drinking thinking plays a big role in bingeing. Do you rationalize heavy drinking because you feel frustrated? Deprived? Bored? Or you need to be "bad" once in a while—because you're so "good" most of the time?

This kind of thinking—drinking thinking—gets you in hot water. So it's only logical to tackle it. Next time you're grappling with drinking thinking, use the tips you've learned to direct it—and avoid bingeing.

Poke holes at the logic behind it. Is alcohol a sensible solution to feeling deprived, bored, frustrated, or rebellious? Of course not!

Replace it with positive inner conversation when you catch yourself thinking this way. Look back on your past accomplishments in the program—you can make a difference in your drinking behavior! And look forward to a great future when you won't have to worry about embarrassing bingeing. Remind yourself of nonalcoholic rewards you've planned for taking charge of drinking thinking and successfully beating the bingeing urge.

Look for logical solutions to feelings that lead you to drinking thinking and bingeing. Bored? Dream up something exciting to do. Frustrated? Acknowledge those feelings and problem-solve the issues.

Want to be "bad" for a change? Dye your hair green, dress down, or eat everything in sight that's usually off limits. You'll be breaking the rules but not putting yourself or others at risk with too much alcohol.

Long-term solutions to feelings and drinking thinking may cure you of the bingeing urge. And if all else fails, "get a grip"—and just stop drinking. So simple!

Direct your drinking thinking and you'll tame the bingeing urge.

Play With the External Variables Too You know how to
direct and control drinking thinking. Now take control of
the people, places, and circumstances that might get you in
drinking trouble too.

When you're feeling the bingeing urge coming on, try to
steer clear of drinking companions who might give you
their "silent permission" to get drunk.

Or avoid the same old watering hole that has been the
scene of so many of your bingeing nightmares. A change of
scenery could help you avoid a bingeing response. Think
about it!

And if you're drawn to alcohol at a certain time of day,
that's easy. Distract, distract, distract. You've got a lot of
interesting things you've already planned for that time of
the day, haven't you?

Modifying the external cues will interrupt your bingeing
cycle in the action stage.

Do You Remember How Foolish You Felt After Bingeing?
Now, there's a powerful deterrent to bingeing and a motivating factor to break your drinking cycle!

When was the last time you went all out and got drunk?
Can you remember? Or did you black out—and hear about
your escapades the next day?

Remind yourself of the horrible hangover, how ashamed
and embarrassed you felt the day after. And how you alien-
ated family and friends when you were intoxicated—if that's
the case.

These memories could make the difference between making your moderate-drinking goal or living with bingeing the
rest of your life.

Your Last Resort? Compromise! So you're fighting this
uncontrollable urge to binge. And it seems as if nothing you
say or do is working to manage it.

Compromising with yourself might be in order. Okay—
you won't stay within your drink limits for the day. But does

that mean you have to get drunk and pass out? Of course not!

Allow yourself one or two over your limit. Just make sure you're not putting yourself or anyone else in danger—especially if you're driving. Call a cab. Stay the night. Whatever.

Maybe compromising will get the urge out of your system, and you won't make a complete idiot of yourself.

Karin Beat Bingeing—and So Can You!

Remember Karin? One of our classic binge drinkers? With determination and hard work, she overcame the bingeing syndrome and met her safe-drinking goal.

Before she faced a potential bingeing situation, she did a lot of soul searching—digging into the feelings and thoughts behind it. Even though she seemed to have the perfect life to most of us, she realized there were some things that were not so perfect—which triggered her bingeing reaction.

Her husband was always on her back about her drinking and trying to keep her in line with what he thought were sensible drinking "rules." In spite of his good intentions, she developed a rebellious attitude toward him. And she knew her overdrinking drove him up a wall.

Most of the time she considered herself a responsible wife and mother—too responsible, she sometimes thought. Wasn't she entitled to a good time every now and then? She spent most of her time concentrating on making her husband and children happy. Didn't she deserve some fun too?

The other obstacle to overcoming her uncontrollable drinking? Girlfriends she had known since high school. They had been drinking buddies for fifteen years, and when they got together, it was just like old times. They'd drink, talk, and listen to music for hours on end—and wind up drunk and hungover the next day. Those friends and drinking parties contributed to her downfall.

Her rebellious attitude and her drinking thinking were the first thinking stages of her bingeing cycle. So she decided to counter them, giving herself as much pampering and attention as she gave everyone else. And she pursued activities that she enjoyed but put off because she was so busy fulfilling her roles as perfect wife and mother.

She also had a heart-to-heart talk with her husband to let him know that the more he kept tabs on her drinking, the more rebellious she became.

She talked to her girlfriends too, clearing the air about their long-term abuse of alcohol and suggesting they grow up. Sure, they could enjoy moderate drinking, but did they always have to go overbroad the way they did fifteen years ago in high school?

A passionate motivational pep talk was always on her agenda—especially if she faced a high-risk drinking party with her old pals. She sat quietly for ten to fifteen minutes to review her reasons for wanting to eliminate overdrinking—so she could be an even better role model for her children, feel better about herself, and not worry about continuing the substance abuse legacy in her family.

Then she programmed herself with a solid drinking plan of action, knowing exactly how much and how long she'd drink and how she'd beat the overdrinking urge when she arrived at the party.

First she reviewed all of the behavior management skills she'd learned, refreshing her memory about which ones worked for her. Then she anticipated and visualized the situation, thinking of the feelings, thoughts, and people that tripped her bingeing response, and directing her drinking thinking, defusing its power and her reaction to it.

Next, she precisely preplanned her drinking behavior. Remember the Basics? One-drink per hour, three drinking hours max, and eating with drinking? This was always helpful to keep in the back of her mind.

She decided on a three-drink limit. She'd snack and alternate with nonalcoholic drinks throughout the party—keeping her BAC down. No gulping and no carrying the drink with her everywhere. She'd focus on the fun and friends—not alcohol.

When the going got tough, she'd treat herself to some stirring positive inner conversation—thinking about her reasons to stay within her drink limit and eliminate bingeing. Four or five hours would be more than enough time for a good visit. And she'd wrap up the party with a latte.

And if she was really tempted to give in and go overboard, she'd talk to her buddies about the importance of cutting her drinking and sticking to the moderation program. Would they like to practice the program too?

Finally, she'd leave if she found it too difficult to control her thinking and feelings. She'd simply "get a grip" and go home so she wouldn't have to worry about going hog-wild at such a high-risk party.

She rehearsed her drinking plan in her head. And most important, she followed through. And stuck to her limit!

She was proud of herself. Her husband was proud of her too. She knew that if she could manage her drinking and beat the bingeing urge just one time, she could do it again and again.

These moderation tools and information helped her plan the perfect drinking party. No guilt or hangover the next day!

Are You Breaking Your Drinking Cycle and Fixing Your Personality?

Have you put all of the pieces of your drinking puzzle together? Do you know the internal and external variables triggering your urge inside out, according to your Drinking Diary? Have you identified a dominant problem-drinking personality?

Interrupting your drinking cycle is as easy as 1-2-3. You can visualize, reflect, and break the cycle—by plugging in all the short-term and long-term Drink/Link Behav-

ior Management Skills you've learned to any thinking or
action stage.

Making important lifestyle and attitude adjustments makes
you less vulnerable to your particular problem-drinking
style. So follow through with your long-term lifestyle plan of
action—enjoy safe, moderate drinking forever!

During the Week

Do you remember your pot of gold at the end of the rainbow—a healthier, happier life? Are your Drinking Diary and
Drink Graph current? Are you treating yourself for sticking
with your drinking plan of action?

Are your "self-control" muscles getting bigger and
stronger every day? Feeling more confident and in control
than you have in a long time?

Just complete your "What's Your Drinking Personality?"
Teaser midweek. And think how great you'll feel when you
accomplish your safe drinking goal.

Week Six: "What's Your Drinking Personality?" Teaser

What's your dominant problem-drinking personality?

What does your problem-drinking cycle look like? Draw
a diagram of it. What specific internal and external cues
trigger it?

How will you break your problem-drinking cycle and beat
the urge with the behavior management skills you've

learned? Which skills will you use in the thinking stages of the cycle? In the action stages of the cycle?

What long-term lifestyle and attitude adjustments are on your agenda to fix your problem-drinking personality?

When was the last time you gave in to your problem-drinking personality? Describe the circumstances.

Now devise a drinking plan of action for the last time you gave in to your old drinking personality. And keep it handy when faced with your next high-risk drinking party.

What drinking challenges do you have coming up in the week ahead?

How will you handle them? Describe your drinking plans of action.

8

WEEK SEVEN: Learn From Your Drinking Mistakes and Enjoy Lasting Success!

"Never give in. Never give in. Never give in," were Winston Churchill's immortal words during World War II. These should be yours too when faced with a slip from your new safe-drinking behavior.

Keep in mind that slipping back to your old drinking routine is part of the process of change. Expect it! You'll probably lapse at least three or four times before you feel completely comfortable and confident moderating.

Practice makes perfect, though! The more you practice your healthy new drinking skills, the more natural and deeply ingrained they become. So "never give in" to old behavior patterns just because you slip off track now and then.

There are three types of drinking "mistakes" you might experience. A "slip" is an isolated incident in which you revert back to your old problem-drinking pattern. A "relapse" is a series of slips. You feel out of control and give in to your heavy-drinking ways for a week or two. And "giving up" is throwing in the towel, losing hope of improving your drinking behavior, and reverting back to your reckless-drinking routine permanently.

If you learn from your drinking mistakes, you'll never have to worry about giving up. So listen up. How you handle a slip or relapse could spell the difference between success and failure in the program and maintaining your moderation goal permanently.

Take Advantage of a Slip

You can look at a slip a couple of different ways—positive or negative.

You could think you're a total failure—incapable of changing or moderating for the long term. You could feel guilty, ashamed, and bad about yourself, just fueling your desire to drink.

Or you could take advantage of a slip—viewing it as your golden opportunity to learn. Learn more and better ways to beat your urge, decrease your chances of slipping again, and increase your chances of maintaining risk-free drinking permanently.

You have choices. You can either get back on the moderation track and feel good about yourself, or you can wallow in guilt and self-pity and give in to your old heavy-drinking ways and alcoholism.

Is slipping the worst thing that can happen to you? No! Slipping and not learning from your mistake is!

The Mistake "Prescription"—Curing Your Drinking Blues

How do you learn from your drinking mistakes? You play detective. You visit the scene of the crime—review the over-drinking episode—then pinpoint the variables that triggered your overdrinking response.

You preplan and program yourself with a safe-drinking plan of action the next time you're faced with a similar set of circumstances. And you follow through with your plan when called for.

The same type of high-risk drinking event that got you into trouble before turns into a low-risk one when you review, pinpoint, preplan, and follow through the next time around.

Solving your overdrinking "mysteries" with this simple four-step formula—your mistake "prescription"—will pull you through tough times and help you stick to the program.

You may have already slipped a couple of times over the seven-week program. Make the most of these mistakes now.

Review the circumstances—internal and external variables tripping your urge. What were your feelings, your thoughts, and the circumstances pushing your drinking buttons?

And what can you do in the future to eliminate or modify these cues or your reaction to them—and avoid falling back to your old drinking habits?

Cheer up! You'll never suffer from the drinking blues again—with your mistake prescription.

More Tips to Learn From a Drinking Mistake

Go Easy on Yourself

Alexander Pope said, "To err is human; to forgive divine." You're only human, but now you can be divine!

We all make mistakes every day. If we were crushed by all of our shortcomings, we'd never accomplish a thing. And the world would be in bad shape.

Stay cool! Be patient and forgiving when you give in to the urge—instead of browbeating yourself. The sooner you acknowledge you slipped and forgive yourself, the sooner you can get back on track and get back to moderating.

So the next time you make a mistake, pick yourself up, dust yourself off, and start all over again. That's the spirit!

Your Antidote to a Slip?
The Mistake Prescription!

1. Review the circumstances of the slip.

2. Pinpoint the variables that got you in trouble and caused you to overdrink.

3. Devise a drinking plan of action when faced with similar high-risk drinking events in the future.

4. Follow through with your safe drinking plan of action when challenged by a similar event.

Reflect on Your Changing Drinking Behavior

If you're suffering from the ups and downs of behavior change, pay attention. Ups and downs, good days and bad days, are normal stages of any behavior change.

Patience is a virtue and you'll have this virtue down by the time you've reached your safe-drinking goal. So keep plugging away and keep plugging in the Drink/Link Behavior Management Skills.

Changing drinking habits and attitudes can be a rocky road. But it's worth it!

Avoiding a Mistake Is Lots Easier Than Fixing One

Look into your crystal ball. What drinking events in your future could be potential disasters for you?

Think ahead. Do hard-drinking buddies trigger your urge? Is drinking thinking your downfall? Free time your worst enemy?

You're an intelligent adult and you've got to use your common sense and evaluate every future drinking occasion—if it's high-risk and if you should be extra vigilant—and devise a solid plan of action to deal with it so that you come out a winner.

If your drinking ain't broke, you don't have to fix it!

Do You Set Yourself up for a Slip—Without Even Knowing It?

There are certain high-risk feelings, thoughts, and circumstances that can make you more susceptible to a lapse than usual.

And the Twelve Step people have summed up those times beautifully with the acronym HALT. That is, when you're too Hungry, Angry, Lonely, or Tired, you're more likely to go overboard, drink too much, and make a drinking mistake.

When you're experiencing extreme emotional and physical states, you're setting yourself up for a slip—so watch it! Recognizing and dealing with these states appropriately will defuse their power over your drinking behavior.

Appropriate ways of dealing with them? Eat or drink a nonalcoholic beverage if you're hungry or need an energy blast. Snooze if you're tired. Practice relaxation techniques if you're wound up. Or problem-solve if emotions are getting the best of you. And get out, get involved in an activity you're interested in, and socialize if you're lonely.

These are healthy ways to deal with internal and external drinking triggers. Not unhealthy ways—like turning to alcohol to feed your hunger, soothe your anger, provide company, or give you a lift.

How many times do you fall into the overdrinking trap when you're hungry or tired? When you feel lonely or bored? Or when you're angry? Check out your Drinking Diary.

Make the Most of Your Huge Repertoire of Drink/Link Behavior Management Skills

You've learned dozens of different behavior management skills—short-term and long-term lifestyle, behavioral, cognitive, and motivational strategies and techniques. And it's up to you to play an active role in shaping your drinking behavior and applying them to your drinking mistakes.

When you slip and have learned the reasons that led to the slip, review all of your behavior management skills. Which ones could you incorporate in your drinking plan of action for the next high-risk drinking event?

Considering all of your behavior management options and putting them to work when needed are cornerstones of Drink/Link and risk-free drinking!

Start Your Drinking Diary and Drink Graph Again

They are great ways to keep you focused and on track! Recording drinking episodes and daily and weekly drink totals and comparing them with past weeks heightens your "drinking awareness" and helps you stay in control.

Do it—if you feel you're slipping too often and want a firmer grip on moderation.

Get Back on Track—No Matter What

You could go round and round with yourself about a drinking mistake.

Your drinking thinking could convince you that drinking a little too much now and then is okay. You've been so good for so long, you're just treating yourself. Or you could be wallowing in guilt and low self-esteem, feeling that you don't have the self-control to follow through with anything you do, so why even try? Drinking thinking at its best!

Stop with the ridiculous reasoning and the negative feelings! Instead of wasting your precious energy putting yourself down and talking yourself into continued heavy drinking, get back on track—today! Wasn't that easy?

Sam and Susan Mastered Their Mistakes—and You Can Too!

Sam and Susan—a married couple—both wanted to do something about their drinking and joined the program. They were extremely successful—they were there for each other for the emotional support they needed during their behavior change.

The program was a breeze for them, and they cut their drinking in half. They underestimated two things, though: how deeply ingrained their old problem-drinking routine was and the psychological effect a slip would have. In fact, they figured they had done so well, they thought they'd never slip and assumed their moderate-drinking habits were permanent.

The second week after they completed the program, they faced a dangerous high-risk drinking occasion. They were attending a party with a number of hard-drinking old pals—other heavy drinkers they'd been socializing with for years.

And they weren't prepared—they felt so comfortable with their new drinking skills, they didn't even bother to program themselves for the party. Mistake!

They drank too much—just like the old days. And woke up with hangovers—physiological and psychological. Between the headaches, stomachaches, and guilt, they thought all was lost. They were devastated at the thought that they'd returned to their problem-drinking ways.

Instead of wallowing in self-pity the Saturday after the party, as soon as they were feeling well enough they reviewed how to handle a slip—to their advantage. Then they reviewed the whole program—refreshing their memories with all the behavior management skills that worked for them.

The first thing they did was practice the mistake prescription. They looked at the internal and external variables causing their overdrinking episode. Where did they go wrong?

Each one had had a long, rough week at work. And they arrived at the dinner party tired and hungry on Friday night. HALT!

They were looking forward to a real bash too—all of their old friends who encouraged excessive drinking were going to be there. Risky drinking cues for anyone.

And each had fallen into the drinking thinking trap. Sam seemed to think he no longer had to worry about his drinking—he had significantly reduced his alcohol consumption and thought he'd succeeded at the program. And Susan felt she owed herself a good time. She had also improved her drinking habits and thought she deserved a treat for her efforts. This thinking translated into drinking as much as she wanted—in the back of her mind.

After they pinpointed the physiological, environmental, and cognitive cues that led to their slips, they started thinking up ways they could handle similar drinking parties in the future—avoiding another drinking disaster and sticking to their limits.

Being hungry and tired when they arrived didn't help. Next time they'd snack beforehand. If possible, they'd squeeze in a catnap before a big drinking party. And instead of starting with Scotch, they'd start with a nonalcoholic soda.

When they did have their first Scotch, they'd watch the clock and pace themselves—making sure not to exceed the one-drink, one-hour Basic and staying under .06 BAC.

Their drinking thinking needed directing too. Sam decided he was overconfident with his new drinking skills. Next time he would not overestimate his ability to handle such an intimidating drinking occasion. And Susan looked at her distorted thinking—the idea of "treating" herself by overdrinking because she had succeeded in the program.

Not logical! She decided to make an extra effort to investigate nonalcoholic rewards if she was inclined to think that way.

Their biggest error, however, was not programming themselves before the dinner party. Programming—and devising a solid plan of action—would have defused many of the high-risk drinking cues and heavy drinking behavior.

Instead of leaving their drinking to chance, they would preplan how much and how long they'd drink. And they would decide on the behavior management skills they'd practice to see them through the next social drinking marathon. Nothing would be left to chance next time.

Dealing with their slip in a positive, patient manner was an important lesson for them. It taught them that there would be ups and downs until their safe new drinking behavior was second nature to them, and that it was normal to feel guilty and ashamed when they fell off the program.

But their drinking mistake had a happy ending in more ways than one. They took advantage of their slip. They learned from it. They increased their self-confidence and self-esteem when challenged by their next high-risk drinking party—knowing where they'd gone wrong in the past and what they could do to ensure success in the future. And they maintained healthy, moderate drinking over the long term—by dealing with their mistakes intelligently.

During the Week

Is your passionate motivational pep talk keeping you focused? Are your Drinking Diary and Drink Graph current? Has programming become effortless?

Are you turning on to natural highs? Rewarding yourself when you make positive behavior changes and staying within your drink limits? Feeling more confident and more in control than ever?

Great! Keep up the good work! And complete your "Master Your Mistakes" Teaser midweek.

Week Seven: "Master Your Mistakes" Teaser

When was your last slip? Describe it. What were the internal and external variables—the physiological and psychological states, peoples, places, or circumstances—that led to it?

How did you handle it when it happened?

How would you handle it now?

What drinking challenges are coming up in the next week?

How will you handle them? Describe your drinking plans of action.

9

Is Moderation Working for You?

Congratulations! You've completed the program. Quite an accomplishment!

Are you feeling on top of the world? Feeling great physically and mentally? Enjoying more self-confidence and self-esteem? Are you more in control of your life than ever? Have your relationships with family and friends improved? How about work—are you getting ahead financially and career-wise? Are you free from worrying about a serious drinking problem and looking forward to all the health benefits of moderation?

These are well-deserved rewards for all your hard work—following through with the program and polishing up a healthy new lifestyle!

Now let's address questions and concerns you might have, clearing any obstacles that might get in the way of your long-term success. Then we'll evaluate your progress. And ask the $64,000 question: Have you made the right drinking decision?

"But I Still Have the Urge to Drink"

Some drinkers think that once they've completed the seven-week Drink/Link program, their desire to drink will be eliminated immediately. In some cases that's true. But most of us will continue to experience some desire to return to our old drinking routine for several months—maybe longer— after we've completed the program.

Practice makes perfect, though! And the more and longer you practice your safe new drinking skills, the less you'll experience your drinking urge.

Your drinking urge will weaken, catching up with your sensible new drinking habits. So decreased desire is coming! It just won't happen overnight. Hang in there!

"But I Don't Get High Enough"

This is another common concern of drinkers in the program. And it may be true for you too—in the beginning.

Heavy drinking may have increased your tolerance to alcohol. Your body has adapted to it over time. The result? You need more and more alcohol to get high. And you won't achieve the same high if you stay within your daily two- or three-drink limit on the program.

The higher your tolerance to alcohol, the more likely you'll have this concern. That's the bad news.

The good news? After you've practiced the program for only three or four weeks—and stayed within your limits most of the time—you will have lowered your tolerance to alcohol.

You'll no longer need four or five drinks to get high, like in the old days. You'll increase your sensitivity to alcohol and enjoy the same high after only two or three drinks!

So stick with the program—you'll need less alcohol to achieve the desired effect. Cutting back will be easier. And lower tolerance will catch up to you too!

"But I Hate to Count Drinks"

You won't have to count drinks forever. Just until your new drinking behaviors have become deeply ingrained and you've lowered your tolerance. Until then, counting drinks is a necessary evil—and helps you stay focused.

How Successful Have You Been?

Wendy started the program averaging about 35 drinks per week. When she completed the program, she was down to 13—a 63 percent reduction in her alcohol consumption and quite a feat!

She felt great. She looked great. And she was ecstatic over the changes she had made over the last seven weeks. She vowed to remain faithful to moderation forever.

Now let's evaluate your success. You don't have to be a math whiz to calculate the reduction in your alcohol consumption. Just follow this simple formula to see how you're doing:

1. Refer to your Drink Graph and add all of your weekly drink totals for the seven-week program. Divide this total by seven. That's your weekly drink average while working the program.
2. Next, estimate the average number of drinks you were drinking per week before you started the program.
3. Subtract the program average from your weekly average before you started the program.
4. Divide the remainder by your weekly average prior to starting the program. This percentage represents the drop in your alcohol consumption over the last seven weeks.

Let's calculate Wendy's progress as an example. Wendy estimated she was drinking around 35 drinks per week before the program.

Then she added up her weekly totals for each of the seven weeks in the program, according to her Drink Graph. The first week she had 28 drinks. Week two she was down to 20. Week three, 12. Week four, 9. Week five, 7! Week six—a little slip—back to 10. Week seven, down to 8! They added up to 94 drinks over the seven-week program.

She divided 94 by 7—giving her 13.42—her average weekly drink total while on the program.

She rounded off to 13 and subtracted it from her 35-drink weekly total prior to the program, giving her 22. Twenty-two drinks less per week!

Then she divided 22 by 35. She rounded off and was amazed at the 63 percent reduction in her alcohol consumption upon completion of the program.

A real coup for Wendy! She exceeded her expectations and cut her drinking more than she thought possible.

Have you cut your drinking by at least 25 percent—hopefully more—since you completed the program? Are you staying within your daily and weekly drink limits most of the time? Are you beating your urge and the nasty little habits that got you into so much trouble in the past?

If you can answer yes to these questions, you get a gold star! You're controlling your drinking and have succeeded in the program!

If you can't answer yes to these questions, have slipped often, and find it difficult to stay within your drink limits or stick to the program, you should consider other options.

More Drink/Link Options—Ensuring Permanent Success!

If you've been moderately successful, but want to reduce your alcohol consumption even more and stay within safe-drinking limits permanently, maybe you could use a helping hand.

Joining or forming a Drink/Link Club in your area might be the secret to your success. Banding together with drinkers who have the same safe-drinking goal you do and enjoying their emotional support might help you achieve and maintain risk-free drinking.

Maybe the Drink/Link Audio Library could give you that extra boost to succeed. Anytime of the day or night, you can get the advice you need to stay on track. Just plug in the audio tape dealing with the topic you're feeling most challenged by and consider the behavior management skills presented.

Confidential Drink/Link Counseling—in person or by phone—offering you personal counseling and prerecorded information might work for you too.

For more information about joining or forming a Drink/Link Club, obtaining a Drink/Link Audio Library or personal counseling, call (707) 539–LINK or write us at P.O. Box 5441, Santa Rosa, CA 95402.

You have a lot of affordable Drink/Link options ensuring your lasting success. Take advantage of them if you need a helping hand.

Abstinence May Be Just
What the Doctor Ordered

Franklin D. Roosevelt said, "It is common sense to take a method and try it. If it fails, admit it frankly and try another. But above all, try something."

Wise advice. If you've tried to moderate and are unable to stay within your daily and weekly limits most of the time, you should be looking into abstinence solutions. They could be easier and more effective for you.

Alcoholics Anonymous—a spiritual approach to sobriety—has helped thousands of people stop drinking. And Rational Recovery and the Secular Organization for Sobriety offer secular, scientific approaches to abstinence.

Your local chapter of the National Council on Alcoholism—listed in your phone book—should have referral numbers for these organizations in your area. Or look in the yellow pages under "Alcoholism Information and Treatment Centers."

You might want to consider professional counseling too if you think it could keep you on the wagon.

Whatever approach you decide, follow through. You've given moderation your best shot. If it doesn't work for you, your next-best solution is stopping drinking altogether. So start investigating abstinence approaches you can live with!

Cheers! To You and Your Intelligent Drinking Decision!

Moderation or abstinence? The $64,000 question! You're an intelligent adult and capable of making the right drinking decision by taking a close look at how much you've cut your alcohol consumption and your ability to maintain your safe new drinking habits permanently.

Drink/Link toasts you, your intelligent drinking decision, and healthy moderation!

We'd Love to Hear From You!

We'd love to know how you're doing. Any and all feedback is welcome, so don't hesitate to write to us. If you'd like, you may include answers to the following questions:

- How much were you drinking before you started this moderation program? What was your average weekly consumption?
- How much are you drinking now that you've completed the program? What's your average weekly consumption now?
- What areas of your life have improved since you've completed the program? Are you feeling better physically? Are you feeling better psychologically—more self-confident and really in control of your life? Are your relationships with family and friends more fulfilling? Has your job performance improved? Is your social life picking up?
- Have family and friends noticed a change for the better in you? What changes have they brought to your attention?
- What were the most helpful parts of the program? The least helpful parts?
- How are you doing—three months, six months, and a year after you've completed the program? Are you maintaining moderate-drinking habits and reduced alcohol consumption?
- Would you be interested in joining or forming a Drink/Link Club in your area? Contact us and we'll con-

nect you with other drinkers with the same moderate-drinking goal.

- Would you be interested in the Drink/Link Audio Library? Contact us and we'll send you more information about it.
- Would you be interested in confidential Drink/Link Counseling? In person or over the phone? Contact us for more information about confidential counseling and prerecorded information designed to keep you on track.

Thanks for you comments and your time.

Sincerely,

D. J. Cornett, M.A.
Founder and Director
The Drink/Link Moderation Program
P.O. Box 5441
Santa Rosa, California 95402
(707) 539-LINK

Bibliography

Alden, L. "Evaluation of prevention self-management programs for problem drinkers." *Canadian Journal of Behavioral Science* 10(3): 258–63, 1978.

_____. "Preventive strategies in the treatment of alcohol abuse: A review and proposal," in Davidson, P. O., and S. M. Davidson, eds. *Behavioral Medicine: Changing Lifestyles*. New York: Brunner-Mazel, 1980.

American Psychiatric Association. *Diagnostic and Statistical Manual of Mental Disorders, 4th ed., rev.* Washington, D.C.: American Psychiatric Association, 1994.

Babor, T. F. "Brief intervention strategies for harmful drinkers: New directions for medical education." *Canadian Medical Association Journal* 143(10): 1070–76, 1990.

_____, and M. Grant, eds. *Programme on Substance Abuse: Project on Identification and Management of Alcohol-Related Problems. Report on Phase II: Randomized Clinical Trial of Brief Interventions in Primary Health Care*, chapter 16. Geneva: World Health Organization, 1992.

_____, et al. "Screening and early intervention strategies for harmful drinkers: Initial lessons from the Amethyst Project." *Australian Drug and Alcohol Review* 6: 325–39, 1987.

_____, E. B. Riston, and R. J. Hodgson. "Alcohol-related problems in the primary health care setting: A review of early intervention strategies." *British Journal of Addiction* 81: 23–46, 1986.

Berg, G., and A. Skuttle. "Early intervention with problem drinkers," in Miller, W. R., and N. Heather, eds., *Treating Addictive Behaviors: Processes of Change*. New York: Plenum, 1986.

154

Bois, C., and M. D. Vogel-Sprott. "Discrimination of low blood alcohol levels and self-triation skills in social drinkers." *Quarterly Journal of Studies on Alcohol* 85: 86–97, 1974.

Burns, D. *The Good Feeling Handbook*. New York: William Morrow, 1989.

Cellucci, T. "The prevention of alcohol problems," in Miller, P. M., and T. D. Nirenberg, eds., *Prevention of Alcohol Abuse*. New York: Plenum, 1984.

Chaney, E., M. O'Leary, and G. A. Marlatt. "Skill training with alcoholics." *Journal of Consulting and Clinical Psychology* 46(5): 1092–1104, 1978.

Cummings, C., J. Gordon, and G. Marlatt. "Relapses: prevention and prediction," in Miller, W., ed. *The Addictive Behaviors: The Treatment of Alcoholism, Drug Abuse, Smoking and Obesity*. Oxford: Pergamon, 1980.

Dean, J. C., and G. A. Poremba. "The alcoholic stigma and the disease concept." *International Journal of Addiction* 18: 739–51, 1983.

Drummond, D. C., et al. "Specialist versus general practitioner treatment of problem drinkers." *Lancet* 336(8720): 915–18, 1990.

D'Zurilla, T., and M. Goldfried. "Problem solving and behavior modification." *Journal of Abnormal Psychology* 78(1): 107–26, 1971.

Edwards, G., J. Orford, and S. Egert. "Alcoholism: A controlled trial of treatment and advice." *Journal of Studies on Alcohol* 38(5): 1004–1031, 1977.

Elal-Lawrence, G., P. Slade, and M. Dewey. "Predictors of outcome type in treated problem drinkers." *Journal of Studies on Alcohol* 47(1): 41–47, 1986.

Fingarette, H. *Heavy Drinking: The Myth of Alcoholism as a Disease*. Berkeley, Cal.: University of California Press, 1988.

Heather, N. "Psychology and brief interventions." *British Journal of Addiction* 84(4): 357–70, 1989.

———, and I. Robertson. *Controlled Drinking*. London: Methuen, 1981.

————, J. Kisson-Singh, and G. W. Fenton. "Assisted natural recovery from alcohol problems: Effects of self-help manual with and without supplementary telephone contact." *British Journal of Addiction* 85(9): 1177–85, 1990.

————, B. Whitton, and I. Robertson, "Evaluation of a self-help manual for media-recruited problem drinkers: Six month follow-up results." *British Journal of Clinical Psychology* 25: 19–34, 1986.

Jaffe, D., and C. Scott. *Self-Renewal: A Workbook for Achieving High Performance and Health in a High-Stress Environment.* New York: Simon & Schuster, 1984.

Lloyd, R., and H. Salzberg. "Controlled social drinking: An alternative to abstinence as a treatment goal for some alcohol abusers." *Psychological Bulletin* 82(6): 815–42, 1975.

Marlatt, G. "The controlled drinking controversy." *American Psychologist*, October 1983.

Marlatt, G. A. "Research on behavioral strategies for the prevention of alcohol problems." *Contemporary Drug Problems* 15: 31–45, 1988.

Marlatt, G., and W. George. "Relapse prevention: Introduction and overview of the model." *British Journal of Addiction* 79: 261–73, 1984.

Miller, W. R. "Behavioral treatment of problem drinkers: A comparative outcome study of three controlled drinking therapies." *Journal of Consulting and Clinical Psychology* 46(1): 74–86, 1978.

Miller, W. "Controlled drinking: A history and critical review." *Journal of Studies on Alcohol* 44: 68–83, 1983.

Miller, W. R. "Teaching responsible drinking skills," in Miller, P. M., and T. D. Nirenberg, eds. *Prevention of Alcohol Abuse.* New York: Plenum, 1984.

————. "Techniques to modify hazardous drinking patterns," in Gallanter, M., ed. *Recent Developments in Alcoholism*, vol. 5. New York: Plenum, 1987.

————, and L. M. Baca, "Two year follow-up of bibliotherapy and therapist-directed controlled drinking training for problem drinkers." *Behavior Therapy* 14: 441–48, 1983.

Miller, W., and G. Caddy. "Abstinence and controlled drinking in the treatment of problem drinkers." *Journal of Studies on Alcohol* 38: 986–1003, 1977.

Miller, W. R., C. J. Gribskov, and R. L. Mortell. "Effectiveness of a self-help control manual for problem drinkers with and without therapist contact." *International Journal of Addiction* 16: 827–37, 1981.

———, and R. K. Hester. "Matching problem drinkers with optimal treatments," in Miller, W. R., and N. Heather, eds. *Treating Addictive Behaviors*. New York: Plenum, 1986.

———, and R. Hester. "Treating the problem drinker: Modern approaches," in Miller, W., ed. *The Addictive Behaviors: The Treatment of Alcoholism, Drug Abuse, Smoking and Obesity*. Oxford: Pergamon, 1980.

Miller, W., and M. Joyce. "Prediction of abstinence, controlled drinking and heavy drinking outcomes following behavioral self-control training." *Journal of Consulting and Clinical Psychology* 47(4): 773–75, 1979.

———, and D. Matthews. "Estimating blood alcohol concentration: Two computer programs and their applications in therapy and research." *Addictive Behaviors* 4: 55–60, 1979.

———, and R. Munoz. *How to Control Your Drinking*, rev. ed. Albuquerque: University of New Mexico, 1990.

Miller, W. R., and C. A. Taylor. "Relative effectiveness of bibliotherapy, individual and group self-control training in the treatment of problem drinkers." *Addictive Behaviors* 5: 13–24, 1980.

———, C. A. Taylor, and J. C. West. "Focused versus broad-spectrum behavior therapy for problem drinkers." *Journal of Consulting and Clinical Psychology* 48(5): 590–601, 1980.

Orford, J., E. Oppenheimer, and G. Edwards, "Abstinence or control: The outcome for excessive drinkers two years after consultation." *Behavior Research and Therapy* 14: 409–418, 1976.

Persson, J., and P. H. Magnusson, "Early intervention in patients with excessive consumption of alcohol: A controlled study." *Alcohol* 6(5): 403–408, 1989.

Pomerleau, O., M. Pertschuk, and J. Stinnet. "A critical examination of some current assumptions in the treatment of alcoholism." *Journal of Studies on Alcohol* 37(7): 849–67, 1976.

Prochaska, J. O., and C. C. DiClemente. "Toward a comprehensive model of change," in Miller, W. R., and N. Heather, eds. *Treating Addictive Behaviors*. New York: Plenum, 1986.

Rohsenow, D. J., R. Smith, and S. Johnson. "Stress management training as a prevention program for heavy social drinkers: Cognitions, affect, drinking, and individual differences." *Addictive Behaviors* 10: 45–54, 1985.

Rossellini, G., and M. Worden. "The problem drinking continuum," in *Patterns of Use and Abuse*. Tempe, Arizona: DIN Publications, 1990.

Ruzek, J. *The Drinkwatchers Handbook*. London: Accept Publications, 1983.

_____. "The Drinkwatchers experience: A description and process report on services for controlled drinkers," in Stockwell, T., and S. Clement, eds. *Helping the Problem Drinker: New Initiatives in Community Care*. London: Croom Helm, 1987.

Sanchez-Craig, M. "Brief didactic treatment for alcohol and drug-related problems: An approach based on client choice." *British Journal of Addiction* 85(2): 169–77, 1990.

_____, et al. "Random assignment to abstinence and controlled drinking: Evaluation of a cognitive-behavioral program for problem drinkers." *Journal of Consulting and Clinical Psychology* 52(3): 390–403, 1984.

_____, D. A. Wilkinson, and K. Walker. "Theory and methods for secondary prevention of alcohol problems: A cognitively-based approach," in Cox, M., ed. *Treatment and Prevention of Alcohol Problems: A Resource Manual*. New York: Academic Press, 1984.

U. S. Departments of Agriculture and Health and Human Services. *Dietary Guidelines for Americans—Fourth Edition*. Washington, D.C.: Supt. of Docs., U.S. Govt. Print. Off., 1995.

U.S. Department of Health and Human Services. *Alcohol Alert—Alcohol and the Liver*. Washington, D.C.: Supt. of Docs., U.S. Govt. Print. Off., 1993.

_____. *Alcohol Alert—Assessing Alcoholism*. Washington, D.C.: Supt. of Docs., U.S. Govt. Print. Off., 1991.

_____. *Alcohol Alert—College Students and Drinking*. Washington, D.C.: Supt. of Docs., U.S. Govt. Print. Off., 1995.

_____. *Alcohol Alert—Moderate Drinking*. Washington, D.C.: Supt. of Docs., U.S. Govt. Print. Off., 1992.

_____. *Alcohol Alert—Screening for Alcoholism*. Washington, D.C.: Supt. of Docs, U.S. Govt. Print. Off., 1990.

_____. *Alcohol Alert—Treatment Outcome Research*. Washington, D.C.: Supt. of Docs., U.S. Govt. Print. Off., 1992.

_____. *Seventh Special Report to the U.S. Congress on Alcohol and Health*. Washington, D.C.: Supt. of Docs., U.S. Govt. Print. Off., 1990.

_____. *Eighth Special Report to the U.S. Congress on Alcohol and Health*. Washington, D.C.: Supt. of Docs., U.S. Govt. Print. Off., 1993.

Vaillant, G. *The Natural History of Alcoholism*. Cambridge, Mass.: Harvard University Press, 1983.

Vogel-Sprott, M. D. "Self-evaluation of performance and the ability to discriminate blood alcohol concentrations." *Journal of Studies on Alcohol* 36: 1–10, 1975.

Vogler, R., J. Compton, and T. Weissbach. "Integrated behavior change techniques for alcoholics." *Journal of Consulting and Clinical Psychology* 45(2): 233–43, 1977.

Vogler, R. E., T. A. Weissbach, and J. V. Compton, "Learning techniques for alcohol abuse." *Behaviour Research and Therapy* 15: 31–38, 1977.

Index